Enola & Prudhomme's

To Mickie

Enjoy Cajun Eating

[signatures]

Cajun Cafe

Also by Enola Prudhomme:

Enola Prudhomme's Low Calorie Cajun Cooking
Enola Prudhomme's Low-Fat Favorites

Library of Congress Cataloging-in-Publication Data
Prudhomme, Enola

ISBN: 0-9658651-0-X

Printed in the USA by

WIMMER
The Wimmer Companies
Memphis

Dedication

I would like to dedicate this book to my sister, Darlee. Darlee was more than a sister—she was like a mother to me. She was always ready to help me in any way she could, even making my clothes for special events or just for me to have something new. I remember how she took care of me when I had my first child. It breaks my heart to see her today as she is in the nursing home and has Alzheimer's. Darlee does not recognize me anymore but I will never forget the way she once was and her helping hand.

I love you, Sis

Acknowledgments

To anyone who loves to cook and can appreciate the hard work that goes into writing recipes. Believe me, they do not get prepared, tested and written by themselves.

I would like to thank Sandra Day for spending long days filled with work, fun, tea and pies! Thanks, Sandra.

To Annette, my daughter, who has been my helping hand from Book One, who learned all about editing, re-editing and re-editing and typing in just the nick of time.

To Liz, my granddaughter, who learned about computers, typing, recipes and everything that goes into writing a cookbook for the very first time.

To Jason, my grandson, who was in a car accident and, thank God, walked away with only a broken arm. He was a great help running back and forth for things needed between the restaurant and test kitchen.

To Howard "*Poonie*" Thomas, the chief custodian in the restaurant. I know at times it was hard but whenever I needed pots and pans cleaned in a hurry, Poonie came through!

To Sonny, Chris, Donald and their wives, who worked their regular jobs and still found time to write and help prepare their recipes.

To my husband, Shelton, who will always see that everything is packed for my book autographing and demos!

Thanks to all of you, because without everyone's help and effort, this book would not have been possible.

Table of Contents

Notes from
Enola's Kitchen for Beginners

Andouille—A popular Cajun smoked pure pork sausage.

Bisques—A thick, rich Cajun soup, bisque is usually made with crawfish, shrimp or crabmeat.

Browning and seasoning sauce—Kitchen Bouquet is used to make the gravy or stew's color darker.

Canned diced tomatoes with green chilies—Rotel tomatoes

Crabmeat—Fresh lump crabmeat is the only seafood I use that is precooked. It is readily available in supermarkets and seafood stores, usually in a 1-pound plastic container. Before using crabmeat in any recipe, be sure to pick through it to remove any stray pieces of shell or cartilage.

Crawfish—Crawfish are plentiful throughout Louisiana and sometimes you can find them in your local supermarkets. If you can't find crawfish, substitute shrimp.

Green onions—Cajuns prefer the term green onions to scallions and we use plenty of them in our cooking. We grow them year 'round in our backyards so we always have plenty on hand.

Campbell's condensed beef broth double-rich double-strength soup—This is a very good broth but remember when using in recipes, that broth also contains salt.

Hot pepper sauce—We use Magic Pepper Sauce by Chef Paul Prudhomme. If this kind is not available to you, you may use your favorite.

Jambalaya—A Cajun dish made with any meat or seafood with lots of seasoning and cooked rice. A great way to use leftovers, bits and pieces of ham, sausage, chicken, etc.

Julienne—To cut in strips.

Lemon-lime carbonated water—7-Up or Sprite.

Maque Choux—A sweet seasoned corn dish using a little cream, chicken, shrimp or crawfish can be sautéed with the corn.

Mildly hot and sweet sauce—Tiger Sauce is what we use. If this sauce is not available to you, you may use another type that is similar.

Mirliton—This gourd-like fruit is about the size and shape of a very large pear and is also know as the chayote or vegetable pear. In South Louisiana, however, it is better known as the mirliton. Look for small, firm, unblemished fruit.

Pasteurized process cheese—We use Velveeta cheese but you may use your favorite cheese.

Rabbit—Use fresh domestic rabbit when possible. Dishes made with rabbit are growing in popularity because rabbit is low in calories and fat.

Roux—Is an equal combination of oil and flour that is cooked to a reddish brown or darker color. Roux is used in gumbos and stews and can also be used as a thickening agent.

Roux Flour—By simply browning the flour in a skillet, you can achieve the same flavor as a traditional roux. Once the roux is made, if stored in a tightly covered container, roux flour will keep for several months.

Seafood, vegetable, and meat seasoning blend—Is Paul Prudhomme's Magic Seasoning. It is sold in most large supermarkets or can be ordered in New Orleans, La. throughout K–Paul's enterprise. You may substitute with Enola's Special Seasonings. (See recipe in Cookbook)

Shrimp—While fresh-from-the Gulf shrimp are always available in South Louisiana, any of these recipes can be prepared with shrimp found in your local market.

Tasso—An intensely smoked Cajun ham that is very highly seasoned.

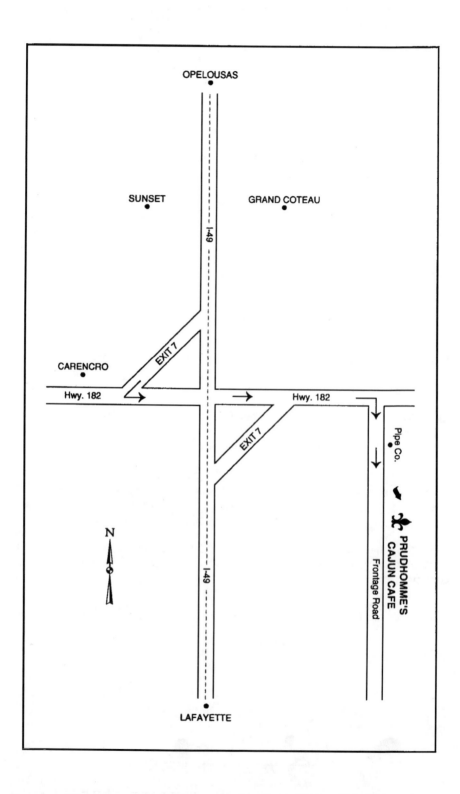

Introduction

Years have come and gone. It is mostly the years that have gone that we remember. So in this introduction we would like to take you back a few years.

Enola Prudhomme

Enola Prudhomme, one of the leading restaurateurs, was born to Mr. and Mrs. Eli Prudhomme in Opelousas, Louisiana. She was reared along with eleven brothers and sisters and attended Academy of the Immaculate Conception in Opelousas.

She grew up on a thriving farm in the bayou country where food was plentiful and she learned at a very young age the art of hard work. Because of the nine brothers and two sisters, one soon realizes the tremendous amount of food which had to be prepared.

Of course, her mother was an excellent cook and Enola remembers watching, helping and learning as she developed a special love for cooking. Little did she realize that this was preparing her to become a famous chef and owner of her very own restaurant.

She seemed to have fallen right into the footsteps of her famous, internationally known brother, Paul Prudhomme. In 1985, she opened her restaurant in historical Washington, Louisiana. It was not very long, however, before the place seemed too small and Enola was looking for something larger. Call it fate, if you will, but she found a beautiful old home, built in the 1800's which seemed to beckon for the restaurant to take up residency and to make it come alive. So...Enola purchased it and moved.

It's been life in the fast lane ever since. With a thriving business, Enola keeps a very hectic schedule but has managed to co-author the *Prudhomme's Family Cookbook*, and author her own, *Enola Prudhomme's Low-Calorie Cooking, Enola Prudhomme's Low-Fat Favorites* and also *Prudhomme's Cajun Cafe Cookbook*. For Enola, living life to its fullest is the only way to live.

Sonny Aymond

Chef Sonny Aymond, an accomplished chef for over 11 years, is the dedicated husband of Radonna and father of two sons, Brady and Beau Aymond. His love for cooking and competition encouraged him to enter numerous cooking competitions including the Culinary Classic in Lafayette, Louisiana, where he won numerous gold, silver and bronze medals.

Aymond has also appeared as a guest judge and journeyed to Sweden with Enola in 1989 where he cooked on board the Viking Cruise Line for two weeks. When out of the kitchen, he enjoys fishing, hunting, racquetball and various other outdoor sports.

Aymond, in appreciation, dedicates his recipes to his mother, Chef Enola Prudhomme, and his uncle, Chef Paul Prudhomme. Both provided training and guidance which contributed to Chef Sonny's success.

Enjoy Cajun Eating
Chef Sonny

Chris Oncale

I would like to take this time to introduce myself. My name is Chris Oncale. I am married to Enola's youngest daughter, Annette. We have two children, Leigh Danneille and Christopher James II (C.J.). I was raised in a baking family. My mother and father were the owners of Coonie's Bakery. I worked in the bakery all through school. Being a high school boy and having a family business, working was a way of life. After I graduated from high school I went to work in the oil field business. I quit the oil field because the business was not doing so good. Leaving it was the right thing to do.

Enola took in a derrick hand and really brought out the best of my cooking abilities, abilities I didn't know I had! The second year the restaurant was open, Enola encouraged all the chefs to be in the Culinary Classic.

That year I took home a Gold Medal. Still learning the art of cooking two years later, I was pleased to take home another Gold Medal. So if Enola can teach an oilfield worker to cook and love what he does, if you love to cook, there is no telling what you can do. Hope you enjoy the recipes!

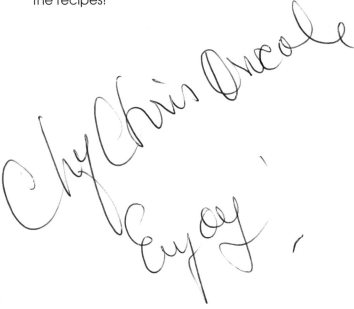

Donald Hebert

Working in the oil field for eight years was hard work but it brought in enough money to support a family. But when the oil business in Louisiana hit bottom, it was time to look for another means of support. So, when I heard about Enola Prudhomme's Cooking School, I eagerly enrolled. I loved to cook and had done most of the cooking at home after I got married.

Soon after finishing the eight-week course, my family and I relocated to another state. There I started my first job as a chef. I soon received numerous job offers. Being away from our families for that long made my wife, Deena, and our four children, Chris, Ashly, Nick and Brad, homesick. So, we made our way back home to Louisiana.

That's how I started to work and became a part of Enola Prudhomme's Cajun Cafe. Enola and her family welcomed my wife and I into her business where we've been for seven years. My name is Chef Donald Hebert and I hope you enjoy the recipes I've contributed to this cookbook.

APPETIZERS

Fried Onion Rings

 Makes 4 appetizer servings

2 eggs, beaten	¼ teaspoon ground red pepper
2 cups canned evaporated milk, in all	¼ teaspoon garlic powder
1¼ cups all-purpose flour	3 large onion, sliced ¼-inch thick and separated into rings
¼ teaspoon baking powder	
1 teaspoon salt	2½ cups vegetable oil
¼ teaspoon ground white pepper	

In a medium bowl, combine eggs, 1½ cups milk, flour, baking powder, salt, white pepper, red pepper and garlic powder. Mix well and set aside. In a small bowl, pour remaining milk. Dip the onion rings into milk, then into the batter. In a 5-quart pot over high heat, heat oil until very hot. Carefully drop the battered onion rings in oil and cook 3 to 5 minutes or until golden brown.

Chef Chris Oncale

Refilled Easter Eggs

Makes 12 halves

 Easter is a wonderful time of year: the fact that it is sacred and spring is in the air and the children have a great time with eggs. This recipe will help you find ways to enjoy leftover Easter eggs. You won't want to wait until the next Easter to enjoy this dish again.

6	hard-cooked eggs	1	tablespoon prepared mustard
¼	cup crispy bacon bits		Paprika
½	cup mayonnaise	12	fresh parsley sprigs

Cut eggs in halves lengthwise. Remove egg yolks and place in small bowl; reserve the egg whites. Using a fork, mash the egg yolks. Add the bacon, mayonnaise and mustard. With a small spoon, fill each reserved egg white with yolk mixture. Sprinkle a dash of paprika on each filled egg, then top each one with a parsley leaf. Great appetizers!

Chef Chris Oncale

Mushroom Cheese Rounds

 Makes 3 dozen appetizers

8 ounces fresh mushrooms, cleaned and sliced	36 garlic-flavored melba toast rounds
1 cup finely chopped onion	1 cup (4 ounces) grated Swiss cheese
1 clove garlic, minced	½ cup (2 ounces) grated Parmesan cheese
1 tablespoon butter or margarine	

Preheat oven to 350 degrees. Place mushrooms, onion, garlic and butter in medium sauce pan over medium heat. Cook and stir 10 minutes. Spoon 1 teaspoon of mixture on each melba toast round and sprinkle each with both cheeses. Arrange in a baking dish. Bake until cheese is melted.

Chef Donald Hebert

Stacie's Shrimp-Stuffed Potatoes

 Makes 40 potato appetizers

2	tablespoons salt	20	small (about 2 ounces each) potatoes
1½	teaspoons ground white pepper	3	tablespoons sour cream
1½	teaspoons ground red pepper	3	tablespoons mayonnaise
1	tablespoon granulated garlic	2	tablespoons chopped pimento
2½	pounds small shrimp, peeled and deveined	1	tablespoon chopped parsley
9	cups water, in all		Small parsley leaves for garnish

In a small bowl, combine salt, white pepper, red pepper and garlic, mixing well. Set aside. Mince ½ pound shrimp and set aside. In a small pot, combine 1 cup water, 1 tablespoon dry seasoning mixture and remaining shrimp. Bring to a boil and cook 5 minutes. Drain and set aside, reserving 40 shrimp. In 5-quart pot, place remaining water and bring to a boil. Scrub potatoes with brush to clean. Add potatoes to boiling water and cook 45 minutes. Potatoes should be cooked but still firm. Remove from heat, drain and set aside to cool. Cut each potato in half. With a melon baller, scoop out center and place in glass bowl. Place potato shells on a tray. Season inside of potato shells with 3 teaspoons seasoning mixture and set aside. To potato pulp, add 2 teaspoons seasoning, sour cream, mayonnaise, minced shrimp, pimento and parsley. With a fork, mash potatoes until smooth. Place mixture in a pastry bag. Fill each potato with shrimp mixture. Place 1 shrimp on each stuffed potato and garnish with a leaf of parsley. Potatoes can be filled with a teaspoon instead of using a pastry bag.

Chef Enola Prudhomme

Boiled Pickled Shrimp

 Makes 8 appetizer servings

4 cups water	2 pounds medium shrimp
1 tablespoon plus 2 teaspoons	(30 to 35 count), peeled
salt, in all	and deveined
1½ teaspoons ground white	1 thinly medium sliced red
pepper, in all	onion
1½ teaspoons ground red	½ cup vegetable oil
pepper, in all	½ cup white vinegar
4 bay leaves, in all	2 teaspoons celery seeds
3 tablespoons pickled spice	2 teaspoons granulated garlic
	Lemon wedges
	Curly parsley sprigs

In a 5-quart pot, combine water, 1 tablespoon salt, ½ teaspoon white pepper, ½ teaspoon red pepper, 2 bay leaves and pickling spice. When water begins to boil, add shrimp. Cook, stirring occasionally, for 8 minutes. Drain, place in a large bowl and set aside. In a glass bowl, combine onion, oil, vinegar, celery seeds, remaining 2 teaspoons salt, 1 teaspoon red pepper, 1 teaspoon white pepper, 2 bay leaves and garlic. Pour mixture over shrimp and stir well. Place in refrigerator 8 hours, stirring occasionally. Remove shrimp from mixture with slotted spoon. Arrange on silver tray. Garnish with lemon wedges and parsley.

Chef Enola Prudhomme

Seafood Stuffed Mushroom Caps

 Makes 4 appetizer servings

Mushrooms:

16 fresh large mushrooms
2 tablespoons butter or margarine
½ cup very finely chopped onion
2 tablespoons very finely chopped green bell pepper
1 teaspoon salt
1 teaspoon ground white pepper
1 tablespoon paprika

1 tablespoon Worcestershire sauce
⅓ cup fresh lump crabmeat, picked over
½ cup chopped, peeled and deveined small shrimp
1 tablespoon heavy whipping cream
¼ cup fine dry bread crumbs
  Vegetable oil

Batter:

2 cups milk
2 eggs

2 cups all-purpose flour

Remove stems from caps. Mince stems, reserving caps for later use. In a medium skillet over high heat, melt butter. Add onion, bell pepper, mushroom stems, salt, white pepper and paprika. Cook and stir 5 minutes. Add Worcestershire sauce, crabmeat, shrimp and cream. Cook and stir 4 minutes. Remove from heat and stir in bread crumbs. Spoon equal amounts of filling in each cap. Beat eggs and milk together to make an egg wash. Dredge stuffed caps in flour, then in egg wash and back in flour. Place in hot oil and fry for about 3 to 5 minutes or until golden brown.

Chef Chris Oncale

Shrimp Puffs

Makes 36 appetizers

 Sometimes use these shrimp puffs on our appetizer trays. It can be prepared ahead of time and refrigerated until ready to fry. If you like your food spicy, add the cayenne. These little puffs are great at a party. Just fry, eat and enjoy!

1 pound small shrimp, peeled and deveined	½ cup all-purpose flour
3 eggs, well beaten	1 cup slightly crushed corn flakes
½ cup heavy whipping cream	2 tablespoons very finely chopped onion
1¼ teaspoons seafood seasoning	¼ cup finely chopped green onion
¼ teaspoon cayenne pepper (optional)	2 cups vegetable oil

Place shrimp in food processor, press pulse button 4 to 5 times or until shrimp are chopped and set aside. In a medium bowl, combine eggs, cream, seafood seasoning, cayenne pepper, flour, corn flakes, onion and green onion, stirring well to mix. Add shrimp and let stand a few minutes for flavor to marinate. In a medium skillet over high heat, heat oil until hot. With a small scoop or spoon, drop mixture carefully into hot oil. Cook 5 or 6 scoops at a time, frying until golden brown, turning often. Remove from skillet with slotted spoon and place on paper towel to drain. Serve hot.

Chef Enola Prudhomme

Barbecued Chicken Wings

 Makes 6 appetizer servings

36 chicken drumettes
¾ cup chicken broth
½ cup Worcestershire sauce
½ cup bottled mildly hot and sweet sauce
½ cup honey

½ cup white vinegar
1 teaspoon salt
1 teaspoon minced garlic
½ teaspoon coarsely ground black pepper

Place chicken wings in a baking dish and set aside. In a medium bowl, combine broth, Worcestershire sauce, hot and sweet sauce, honey, vinegar, salt, garlic and black pepper, mixing well. Pour mixture over chicken. Cover and refrigerate about 30 minutes. Cook chicken on hot grill, turning often, 20 to 25 minutes or until wings are crispy.

Chef Chris Oncale

Cajun Corn Fritters

 Makes 12 to 15 fritters, (about ¾-inch balls)

1	cup self-rising flour	1⅓	cups whole kernel corn
1	teaspoon salt	½	cup evaporated milk
¼	teaspoon ground white pepper	¼	teaspoon hot pepper sauce
1	teaspoon sugar	2½	cups plus 2 teaspoons vegetable oil
2	eggs, beaten		

In medium bowl, add flour, salt, pepper and sugar. Add eggs, corn, milk, the 2 teaspoons oil and the hot sauce; using a wire whisk, mix until smooth.

In a 5-quart pot over high heat, heat the 2½ cups of oil until very hot. With a tablespoon, drop mixture into hot oil. Cook 3 to 5 minutes, or until fritters are golden brown on all sides.

Chef Chris Oncale

Notes

SOUPS
& GUMBOS

Potato and Brie Soup

 *Makes 10 cups*

10 cups beef broth
10 cups diced potatoes, in all
1   cup very finely chopped
    onion
½   cup very finely chopped red
    bell pepper

½   cup very finely chopped
    green bell pepper
1½ teaspoon salt
1   teaspoon minced garlic
½   teaspoon ground white
    pepper
6   ounces brie cheese

Pour broth into a 5-quart pot over high heat and bring to a boil. Add 5 cups potatoes, onions, bell peppers, salt, garlic and white pepper. Cook 15 minutes, stirring occasionally. Remove potatoes, add to food processor along with brie and blend until smooth. Add to soup mixture along with remaining potatoes. Cook an additional 10 minutes or until potatoes are tender and cheese is melted, stirring occasionally. Serve hot.

Chef Enola Prudhomme

Jessie's Favorite Split Pea Soup

Makes 6 servings

 This recipe is named after Enola's youngest great-granddaughter.

½   **pound dry split peas (about 1 cup)**

4   **cups water**

½   **pound ham or tasso, cut in ½-inch cubes (about 2 cups)**

2   **medium carrots, finely chopped**

2   **medium onions, finely chopped**

2   **baking size potatoes, peeled and cut in ½-inch cubes**

½   **cup chopped celery**

4   **teaspoons beef bouillon granules**

1   **tablespoon Enola's Special seasoning**

In an 8-quart pot over high heat, combine all ingredients. Bring to a boil. Reduce heat to low. Cover and cook 1 hour and 15 minutes, stirring occasionally.

Chef Chris Oncale

Emu, Sausage and Tasso Gumbo

Makes 6 servings

 This is a great low-calorie gumbo! Emu is a large ostrich-like bird from Australia with a very lean dark meat. Over the last few years, this bird became very popular in our area. If you would like more information about the Emu, you can call me. I will be glad to share with you what I know.

1	cup chopped onion	2	cups roux flour
½	cup chopped celery	10	cups water, in all
½	cup chopped bell pepper	1½	teaspoons salt
1	pound turkey smoked sausage, cut in bite-size pieces	½	teaspoon ground red pepper
		1	pound emu meat, cut in thin strips
¾	pound turkey tasso, thinly sliced	¼	cup chopped green onion
			Hot cooked rice

Spray the inside of a large pot with vegetable cooking spray and place over high heat. Combine onion, celery and bell pepper in pot. Cook and stir 5 minutes. Add sausage and tasso. Cook and stir for additional 5 minutes. In a small bowl, combine roux flour and 5 cups water. Stir well. Add salt, red pepper and remaining water to the pot. Reduce heat to medium and cook 20 minutes, stirring occasionally. Reduce heat to simmer. Add emu meat and green onion. Cook 3 minutes, remove from heat, cover and let stand 5 minutes. Serve over rice.

Chef Enola Prudhomme

Donald's Chicken, Andouille and Tasso Gumbo

Makes 32 cups

 Leftovers can be frozen in serving portions.

5 quarts water	2 teaspoons ground red pepper
5 pounds chicken leg quarters or 2 (2½ pound) broiler-fryers, cut into serving pieces	1 teaspoon ground black pepper
3 cups chopped onion	2 teaspoons onion powder
1 cup chopped green bell pepper	1 tablespoon garlic powder
	2 pounds chopped andouille
1 cup chopped celery	1 pound chopped tasso
2 tablespoons salt	2 cups dark roux
	Hot cooked rice

In a 10-quart stock pot, combine water, chicken, onion, bell pepper, celery, salt, red pepper, black pepper, onion powder and garlic powder. Bring to a boil. Add andouille and tasso. Cover and return to a boil. Reduce heat to medium. Cook 30 minutes, stirring occasionally. Skim oil off top any time during cooking process and discard. Remove chicken from pot and cool thoroughly. While chicken is cooling, add roux to liquid in pot, stirring until roux is dissolved. Continue to cook over medium heat 15 minutes. Reduce heat to low. Skin and bone chicken; return chicken to pot. Keep warm until ready to serve. Serve over rice in a gumbo bowl.

Chef Donald Hebert

Louisiana Corn Crab Soup

 Makes 6 servings

¼	pound butter or margarine	¾	teaspoon salt
¾	cup finely chopped onion	½	teaspoon cracked black
¾	cup finely chopped red		pepper
	onion	1	teaspoon sugar
¼	cup finely chopped celery	1	(10 ounce) can evaporated
3½	cups heavy whipping cream		milk
5	cups frozen whole kernel	1	teaspoon Worcestershire
	corn		sauce
¼	teaspoon ground red pepper	½	pound lump crab meat,
2	tablespoons finely chopped		picked over
	parsley		

In a 5-quart pot over high heat, combine butter, onion, red onion, and celery. Cook and stir 2 minutes. Add cream and corn. Continue cooking 5 minutes. Add red pepper, parsley, salt and black pepper. Return to a rapid boil. Add sugar and cook 8 minutes. Remove from heat and transfer to food processor. Press pulse button 4 or 5 times. Return mixture to same pot. Stir in the milk and Worcestershire sauce. Cook and stir 3 minutes. Add crabmeat and cook additional 2 minutes. Let stand 5 minutes before serving.

Chef Chris Oncale

Enola's Turtle Soup

Makes 12 servings

 I cooked this soup for a dinner party in New Orleans at the home of Mr. and Mrs. Ronnie Cole. The honoree was Julia Child. The soup looks hard to make but it's worth every bit of your time and every bite! Freeze the leftovers for a cold winter night.... mmmm! C'est Bon!

4	pounds bone-in turtle meat	1	cup finely chopped celery
2	teaspoons lemon pepper seasoning	½	cup finely chopped green bell pepper
2	teaspoons salt	12	cups beef stock or water
1	teaspoon dried basil leaves, crushed	1	(6 ounce) can tomato paste
½	teaspoon dried thyme	1½	cups (12 ounces) tomato sauce
½	teaspoon ground white pepper	3	bay leaves
½	teaspoon ground red pepper	1	garlic clove, minced
4	tablespoons butter or margarine	1	cup finely chopped green onion
⅓	cup all-purpose flour	¼	cup finely chopped fresh parsley
2	cups finely chopped red onion	2	tablespoons fresh lime juice
		⅓	cup dry sherry

In a large bowl, place turtle meat. Sprinkle next lemon pepper, salt, basil, thyme, white pepper and red pepper evenly over the meat and mix well. Set aside to marinate for 1 hour. Melt the butter in a large Dutch oven over high heat. Add the marinated meat, cook and stir 15 minutes or until meat is browned on all sides. Remove the meat and set aside. In the same pot, add butter. Gradually add the flour, stirring constantly and cooking 5 to 8 minutes or until roux turns reddish-brown in color. Return meat to the pot along with the red onion, celery and bell pepper. Continue cooking 15 minutes, stirring to prevent sticking. Add the stock or water, tomato paste, tomato sauce and bay leaves. Reduce heat to medium and cook 1 hour or until meat is tender. Add the garlic, green onion, parsley, and lime juice. Cook an additional 10 minutes. Remove meat from the pot, set aside and let cool to touch. Bone the meat, discarding bones. Cut meat into cubes and return to pot. Add the sherry and cook 1 minute longer. Remove from heat and discard bay leaves before serving.

Chef Enola Prudhomme

Crab and Corn Soup

 Makes 8 servings

8	ears corn on the cob or 2 (16 ounce) packages frozen corn
4	tablespoons butter or margarine
1	cup finely chopped onion
2	stalks celery, finely chopped
¼	cup all-purpose flour

2	(8 ounce) bottles clam juice
1½	pints heavy whipping cream
2	(12 ounce) cans evaporated milk
½	teaspoon salt
1	teaspoon ground red pepper
1	pound lump crabmeat, picked over

If using fresh corn, cut corn from cob and set aside. If using frozen corn, place defrosted corn in food processor and press pause button several times to just break up the kernels. In a large pot over medium heat, melt butter. Add onion and celery. Cook and stir 10 minutes or until onion and celery are transparent. Add flour and blend well. Add clam juice, whipping cream, evaporated milk and corn. Mix well. Add salt and red pepper. Cook and stir 30 minutes. Reduce heat to simmer, add crabmeat and cook an additional 10 minutes.

Chef Sonny Aymond

Chicken, Sausage and Tasso Gumbo

Makes 32 cups

1½ cups plus 2 tablespoons vegetable oil	2 pounds pork andouille sausage, cut in 1-inch pieces
2 cups all-purpose flour	½ pound pork tasso, thinly sliced
3 cups finely chopped onion, in all	16 cups stock or water
1 cup finely chopped bell pepper, in all	1 tablespoon salt
1 tablespoon meat seasoning blend	½ teaspoon ground red pepper
4 pounds chicken breasts, cut in bite-size pieces	½ cup finely chopped green onion
	3 tablespoons very finely chopped parsley
	Hot cooked rice

In large heavy skillet over high heat, heat 1½ cups oil until very hot. Add flour and stir constantly about 10 minutes or until reddish-brown. Add 1 cup onion and ½ cup bell pepper. Reduce heat to medium and continue to cook and stir about 5 minutes. Remove from heat and stir for a few additional minutes to prevent sticking. Stir in meat seasoning. Set roux aside. In large pot over high heat, place remaining oil and heat until very hot. Add remaining onion and bell pepper. Cook and stir 10 minutes. Add chicken, sausage and tasso. Cook and stir 15 minutes. Add stock or water and roux. Cook, stirring occasionally, about 20 minutes. Add salt and red pepper. Cook an additional 10 minutes. Remove from heat. Add green onions and parsley. Let stand 10 minutes, stirring occasionally. Serve over hot rice.

Chef Enola Prudhomme

Radonna's Broccoli Soup

 Makes 6 servings

8	cups water	2½	teaspoons salt
8	cups fresh broccoli florets	⅛	teaspoon ground red pepper
1½	quarts heavy whipping cream	¼	cup unsalted butter
3	cups evaporated milk	½	cup all-purpose flour

In a large pot over high heat, bring water to a boil. Add broccoli and continue to boil 20 minutes. Remove from heat, reserve 1 cup of the water and discard remaining water. Put drained broccoli in a food processor and press the pulse button a few times. Do not overprocess. In a large pot over high heat, bring the whipping cream, evaporated milk and reserved cup of water to a boil. Reduce heat to medium. Add the broccoli, salt and red pepper. Cook and stir 15 minutes. Melt butter in a medium skillet over medium heat. Add the flour and cook, stirring constantly, until flour turns the color of caramel. Remove from heat and slowly add to broccoli mixture until desired thickness.

Chef Sonny Aymond

Potato Soup C.J.

Makes 8 servings

 This recipe will take a little more time than the rest, but the taste will be worth the wait!

½ cup butter or margarine, melted	1 pound tasso, diced
2 cups chopped onion	4 cups wedge-cut potatoes
⅓ cup chopped celery	2 cups milk
1 cup chopped green onion	¼ cup all-purpose flour
1 teaspoon minced garlic	1 (10¾ ounce) can cream of celery soup, undiluted
½ cup chopped green bell pepper	1 (10¾ ounce) can golden mushroom soup, undiluted
12 cups water, in all	¼ cup chopped parsley
6 cups diced potatoes (about ½-inch thick)	½ tablespoon dried basil leaves, crushed
4 cups cubed potatoes	1 tablespoon salt
2 pounds mixed smoked sausage, thinly sliced	2 teaspoons cayenne pepper

In a large pot over high heat, combine butter or margarine, onion, celery, green onion, garlic and bell pepper. Sauté 5 minutes until soft but not browned. In a soup pot, combine 8 cups water and 6 cups diced potatoes. Boil until tender. With the back of a fork, mash potatoes down in water. Add 4 cups cubed potatoes, 4 cups water, sausage and tasso. Cook 20 minutes or until potatoes are tender. Add 4 cups potato wedges and sautéed vegetables. In a small bowl, combine milk and flour, mix well and add mixture to soup. Stir well and cook over medium heat until potatoes are tender. Add cream of celery soup, cream of mushroom soup, parsley and basil, mixing well. Add salt and cayenne pepper. Let simmer 10 minutes to allow flavors to mix together.

Chef Chris Oncale

SALADS

Shrimp Stuffed Tomato

 *Makes 4 servings*

⅔ cup mayonnaise	1 stalk celery, very finely chopped
1 teaspoon salt	
½ teaspoon ground white pepper	2 pounds small shrimp, boiled and peeled
¼ teaspoon ground red pepper	½ cup fine dry bread crumbs
1 small onion, very finely chopped	4 large tomatoes
	Lettuce leaves for garnish
1 small green bell pepper, very finely chopped	Lemon wedges for garnish
	Parsley sprigs for garnish

In a medium bowl, combine all ingredients except tomatoes and garnishes. Mix well. Chill at least 30 minutes. Place tomatoes, stem side up, on cutting board and cut each crossways in quarters, being careful not to cut tomato all the way through. Using a scoop, place equal amounts of mixture inside each tomato. On each 9-inch plate lined with lettuce leaves, place a tomato in the center. Garnish with lemon and parsley. May be served alone as a light lunch or with a nice garden salad.

Chef Chris Oncale

Taco Salad

Makes 2 servings

 While judging a cooking contest in Houston, Texas, I had lunch at a small cafe. I had a dish similar to this and it's dynamite!

Meat Filling:

1	teaspoon chili powder	1	tablespoon vegetable oil
¼	teaspoon salt	½	pound beef flank steak, cut
¼	teaspoon granulated garlic		in ½-inch strips
¼	teaspoon ground red pepper		

Salsa:

2	large tomatoes, peeled, seeded and finely chopped	2	tablespoons very finely chopped green bell pepper
1	very finely chopped fresh jalapeño pepper	2	tablespoons very finely chopped celery
1	clove garlic, minced	1	tablespoon virgin olive oil
2	tablespoons very finely chopped onion		

Salad:

8	large lettuce leaves	2	small tomatoes, peeled, seeded and finely chopped
2	cups torn iceberg lettuce		

For Filling:
Combine first four ingredients in a small bowl. Mix well and sprinkle over meat. Cover and refrigerate at least 4 hours to marinate. In a heavy iron skillet over high heat, heat oil until very hot. Add meat. Cook and stir 10 minutes or until browned. Remove from heat and keep warm.

For Salsa:
In a medium bowl, combine all ingredients and mix well. Cover and refrigerate 1 hour or until chilled.

Assemble:
On each of 2 salad plates, arrange 4 lettuce leaves. Toss together the torn lettuce and tomatoes. Place on leaves and then top with meat. Pour salsa into 2 individual small bowls to serve on side.

Chef Enola Prudhomme

Pretty Strawberry Salad

 Makes 4 servings

⅓ cup vegetable oil	¼ teaspoon ground black
3 tablespoons cider vinegar	pepper
2 tablespoons water	1 head romaine lettuce
1½ tablespoons honey	1 pint fresh strawberries,
1 tablespoon poppy seed	washed, stemmed and
½ teaspoon salt	halved
½ teaspoon paprika	1 small red onion, sliced and
	separated into rings

In a blender, combine oil, vinegar, water, honey, poppy seed, salt, paprika and black pepper. Blend until mixed well. Set aside. Line 4 serving plates with lettuce leaves. Divide strawberries and onion rings among the plates. Stir dressing well, then drizzle over salad and serve.

Chef Donald Hebert

Shrimp and Celery Salad

 Makes 4 servings

2 cups water	2 cups celery, diced
2 teaspoons salt	¾ cup mayonnaise
½ teaspoon ground red pepper	Chopped lettuce
2 pounds small salad shrimp, picked over	

In a medium sauce pan, bring water to a boil. Add salt, red pepper and shrimp. Cook 10 minutes. Drain shrimp and cool in refrigerator 20 to 30 minutes. In a large bowl, mix cold shrimp, celery and mayonnaise together. Serve over bed of chopped lettuce.

Chef Donald Hebert

Cold Sweet Pea Salad

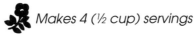 *Makes 4 (½ cup) servings*

4	cups water	2	hard-cooked eggs, coarsely chopped
1	(15 ounce) can sweet peas, undrained	½	cup mayonnaise
½	cup finely chopped onion	2	teaspoons sugar
¼	cup finely chopped green bell pepper	1	teaspoon salt
¼	cup finely chopped celery	¼	teaspoon ground white pepper

In a 4-quart pot, bring water to a boil. Add peas, onion, bell pepper and celery. Cook over medium heat for about 7 minutes. Remove from heat, strain and discard liquid. In a large bowl, combine eggs and cooked mixture. Mix well. Place in refrigerator to cool 30 minutes. Remove from refrigerator. Combine mayonnaise, sugar, salt and white pepper, add to salad and mix well. Cover and refrigerate until ready to serve.

Chef Donald Hebert

Crabmeat Slaw

 Makes 6 (1-cup) servings

8	ounces crabmeat, picked over	2	tablespoons white vinegar
2	cups shredded cabbage	1	tablespoon sugar
½	cup chopped celery	¼	teaspoon salt
1	cup mayonnaise	¼	teaspoon ground red pepper

In a medium mixing bowl, combine crabmeat, cabbage, celery, mayonnaise and vinegar. Mix well. Add remaining ingredients and stir well. Refrigerate 1 hour before serving.

Chef Donald Hebert

Shrimp or Crawfish Warm Salad

 Makes 2 servings

½ head iceberg lettuce	2 tablespoons butter or
6 ounces fresh spinach	margarine
(about ½ a bunch)	1 pound shrimp or crawfish
½ cup diced celery	tails, peeled and deveined
½ cup diced green bell pepper	2 teaspoons Enola's Special
1 medium tomato, quartered	Seasoning
1 hard-cooked egg, cut in	½ cup stock or water
halves	⅛ teaspoon paprika

Tear or cut lettuce and soak in ice water in medium bowl. Remove hard stem from spinach and place in water with lettuce. Drain and pat dry with paper towel. Divide lettuce mixture equally on 2 plates. Add celery and bell pepper on top of lettuce. Place 2 tomato wedges on each salad and set aside. In a medium skillet over high heat, melt the butter. Add shrimp or crawfish and seasoning. Cook and stir 5 minutes or until shrimp turn pink. Add stock and cook 2 minutes. With a slotted spoon, place shrimp on lettuce mixture. Place 1 half egg on each salad. Sprinkle the paprika on the egg. Top with your favorite salad dressing and enjoy.

Chef Enola Prudhomme

Marinated Cucumber and Tomato Salad

 Makes 6 to 8 servings

2	medium cucumbers, peeled and cut in 1-inch slices	¼	teaspoon ground black pepper
2	cups cherry tomatoes, cut in halves	¼	teaspoon ground red pepper
3	cloves garlic, minced	½	teaspoon onion powder
½	cup white vinegar	3	tablespoons vegetable oil
1	teaspoon salt	½	teaspoon Italian seasoning

Place cucumbers and tomatoes in a medium mixing bowl. In another bowl, combine all other ingredients. Pour over cucumber and tomato; gently mix to coat vegetables. Refrigerate 1 hour before serving.

Chef Donald Hebert

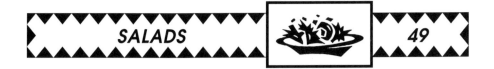

Marinated Crabmeat Salad

 *Makes 4 servings*

1	pound fresh crabmeat, picked over	1	teaspoon salt
1	medium-sized yellow onion, finely chopped	½	teaspoon ground white pepper
1	cup olive oil	1½	cups crushed ice
½	cup white vinegar		Chopped lettuce

In a medium bowl, combine crabmeat and onion. In a small bowl, combine oil, vinegar, salt and white pepper. Pour dressing over crabmeat mixture and top with ice. Cover and refrigerate 8 hours or overnight. Drain salad, serve on a bed of lettuce.

Chef Donald Herbert

Macaroni Salad

Makes 8 servings

 This salad is delicious warm or cold. You can turn it into a main dish by adding boiled shrimp or grilled chicken breast strips.

8   cups water
1   tablespoon salt
3½   cups uncooked macaroni
1   (3 ounce) package cream
     cheese, softened
¼   cup mayonnaise
1   cup thinly sliced celery
½   cup finely chopped red
     onion

½   cup finely chopped green
     bell pepper
½   cup finely chopped red bell
     pepper
½   cup sweet pickle relish
     (optional)
½   teaspoon ground white
     pepper

In a large pot over high heat, bring water and salt to a boil. Add macaroni and cook according to package directions. Drain and place in a large bowl. In a small bowl, combine cream cheese and mayonnaise, mixing well. Add remaining ingredients and mix well. Pour dressing over macaroni and toss to coat well.

Chef Enola Prudhomme

Cool Cucumber Salad Dressing

Makes 3 cups

 Extra dressing can be stored in an air-tight container in the refrigerator for up to 2 weeks.

1	cucumber, peeled and diced	2	tablespoons white vinegar
1	cup mayonnaise	2	teaspoons salt
½	cup sour cream	½	teaspoon ground black pepper
1	(8 ounce) package cream cheese		

Place all ingredients in a blender and blend until smooth. Chill in refrigerator 1 hour before serving. Serve over your favorite salad.

Chef Donald Hebert

Brad's Bacon Blend Salad Dressing

 Makes 4 cups

12 slices bacon	1 cup heavy whipping cream
7 cloves garlic	2 cups mayonnaise
5 medium-sized green hot peppers	1 tablespoon white vinegar
1 (8 ounce) package cream cheese, softened	½ teaspoon salt

In a medium skillet over high heat, fry bacon until crisp. Remove bacon from skillet and place on paper towel to drain. Add garlic and peppers to hot bacon fat. Braise peppers and garlic, turning until evenly browned on all sides. Remove from skillet and place on paper towel to drain. Let peppers and garlic cool. In a food processor, combine bacon, garlic and peppers. Press pulse button 3 or 4 times until bacon, garlic and peppers are coarsely chopped. Add cream cheese, cream, mayonnaise, vinegar and salt. Press pulse button 2 or 3 times. Place dressing in a covered jar and refrigerate for up to 3 weeks.

Chef Donald Hebert

Honey Mustard Dressing

 *Makes 2½ cups*

1¼ cups vegetable oil	2¼ teaspoons granulated garlic
½ cup apple cider vinegar	2 tablespoons black sesame
½ cup honey	seeds
2 tablespoons Grey Poupon mustard	

In a large bowl, combine all ingredients. Mix with a wire whisk or hand mixer at low speed for 1 minute. Serve over salad! Store dressing in refrigerator.

Chef Enola Prudhomme

House Dressing

Makes 7 cups

 This dressing can become a wonderful dip, just add crisp bacon crumbs, bacon bits or chopped ham. Eat with potato chips, crackers or corn chips.

1 small onion, peeled and quartered	4 cups mayonnaise
1 medium-sized green bell pepper, chopped	½ cup sweet relish
1 (3 ounce) package cream cheese, softened	1 tablespoon plus 2 teaspoons Enola's Special Seasoning

In a food processor, place onion and press pulse button off and on until onion is finely chopped. Clean processor and repeat the same process with bell pepper. Place both vegetables in bowl and set aside. Combine cream cheese and mayonnaise in food processor and process until well mixed. Add sweet relish and seasoning; process a few seconds. Add mixture to onion and bell pepper mixture and mix well. Makes a great dressing!

Chef Enola Prudhomme

SEAFOOD

Crawfish Au Gratin

 Makes 4 servings

2	tablespoons butter or margarine, in all
1½	tablespoons all-purpose flour
2	cups finely chopped onion
1½	tablespoons seafood seasoning
3	cups Louisiana crawfish tails

2	cups heavy whipping cream
1	(10¾-ounce) can aged Cheddar cheese sauce
1	tablespoon dry bread crumbs
⅛	teaspoon paprika

Preheat oven to 375 degrees. In a medium skillet, melt 1 tablespoon butter over high heat. Add flour, stirring continuously. Cook and stir 3 to 5 minutes or until roux is the color of peanut butter. In an large heavy sauce pan over high heat, melt the remaining 1 tablespoon butter. Add onion and seasoning. Sauté 5 minutes or until onions are tender. Add crawfish. Cook and stir 3 minutes. Add cream and bring to a boil. Reduce heat. Add cheese sauce and cook and stir until cheese is blended. Add roux and cook an additional 5 minutes or until roux is completely dissolved. Pour into a 12x9x2-inch baking dish and sprinkle with bread crumbs and paprika. Bake 10 minutes or until browned on top.

Chef Sonny Aymond

Shrimp Liz

Makes 4 servings

3	tablespoons butter or margarine, in all	1	medium red bell pepper, julienne
1	pound medium shrimp, peeled and deveined	2	cups peeled and diced tomatoes
1	tablespoon plus 2 teaspoons seafood seasoning, in all	3	tablespoons sliced stuffed green olives (optional)
1	medium onion, sliced	1	bay leaf
1	medium green bell pepper, julienne	½	cup seafood stock or water
		½	cup heavy whipping cream
			Hot cooked rice or pasta

In a large skillet over high heat, melt 2 tablespoons butter. Combine shrimp and 2½ teaspoons seasoning. Cook and stir 5 minutes or until shrimp turn pink. Remove shrimp from skillet, set aside and keep warm. In the same skillet, combine remaining 1 tablespoon butter, onion, bell pepper, tomatoes, olives, bay leaf and remaining 2½ teaspoons seasoning. Cook and stir 10 minutes. Add the stock and cream. Cook and stir additional 10 minutes or until sauce thickens. Return shrimp to skillet and heat 1 minute. Remove from heat, remove bay leaf and serve over rice or pasta.

Chef Enola Prudhomme

Red Bell Pepper Sauce with Crabmeat

 *Makes 2 cups*

4	large red bell peppers	½	cup white wine
3	tablespoon butter or margarine, in all	1	tablespoon Enola's Special Seasoning
2	tablespoons very finely chopped onion	1	teaspoon dried marjoram
4	cloves garlic, minced	½	cup heavy whipping cream
½	cup beef broth	1	pound lump crabmeat, picked over

Place bell peppers on a baking sheet and broil 3 or 4 inches from the heat or until charred on all sides. Cool. Remove skin and seed membrane. In a medium skillet over high heat, melt 2 tablespoons butter. Add roasted pepper, onion and garlic. Cook and stir 5 minutes. Add broth, wine, seasoning, marjoram and cream. Cook and stir 10 minutes or until sauce is thickened. Place in blender and puree. In a medium skillet over high heat combine remaining 1 tablespoon butter and sauce. Cook 5 minutes. Add crabmeat and cook and stir 5 minutes. Serve over grilled, broiled or baked fish.

Chef Enola Prudhomme

Crawfish Corn Maquechoux

 *Makes 4 servings*

2	tablespoons butter or margarine	¼	teaspoon salt
8	ears fresh corn, cut from the cob (about 2½ cups)	¼	teaspoon ground red pepper
1	cup finely chopped onion	3	tablespoons sugar
⅓	cup finely chopped green bell pepper	1	cup heavy whipping cream
⅓	cup finely chopped red bell pepper	¼	cup finely chopped green onion
		1	pound Louisiana crawfish tails
			Hot cooked rice

In a medium sauce pan over high heat, melt the butter. Add the corn, onion, bell pepper, salt and red pepper. Cook and stir 10 minutes. Add sugar, cream and green onion. Cook and stir additional 20 minutes or until corn is tender. Add crawfish and cook an additional 5 minutes. Serve over rice.

Chef Chris Oncale

Broiled Shrimp for Two

Makes 2 servings

 Serve with baked potato or green salad, for a delicious low-fat meal.

½	cup lemon juice	1	teaspoon sweet basil
1½	cups olive oil	¼	teaspoon ground red pepper
2	tablespoons minced garlic	¼	teaspoon salt
1	tablespoon Worcestershire sauce	2	dozen medium shrimp, peeled and deveined
1	teaspoon dried tarragon		

In a medium bowl, combine juice, oil, garlic, Worcestershire sauce, tarragon, basil, red pepper and salt. Mix well and set aside. Place shrimp in 2-inch deep pan. Pour mixture over shrimp and mix well. Place in refrigerator 10 hours or overnight. Remove shrimp from mixture. Place shrimp on flat pan and broil 3 minutes. Spoon mixture over shrimp, turn and broil 4 minutes. Make sure shrimp are pink and firm.

Chef Sonny Aymond

Lee-Lee's Fried Soft-Shell Crabs

 *Makes 4 servings*

4	soft-shell crabs	½	teaspoon granulated garlic
1	tablespoon salt	2	eggs, beaten
1	teaspoon ground white pepper	1	cup evaporated milk
½	teaspoon ground red pepper	1	cup all-purpose flour
		2	cups vegetable oil

Clean crabs by removing face and lungs; wash well. Place on paper towel to dry and set aside. In a small bowl, combine salt, white pepper, red pepper and garlic, mixing well. Sprinkle seasoning mixture evenly over crabs. In a medium bowl, beat together eggs and milk. Dip seasoned crabs in mixture, then dredge in flour, making sure to coat crabs on each side. In a 5-quart pot or frying pan over high heat, heat oil until very hot. Using tongs, carefully place crabs in oil. Cook 3 to 4 minutes or until golden brown on both sides. Drain on paper towel and serve immediately.

Chef Chris Oncale

Cheese Crabmeat Stuffed Jumbo Shells

Makes 4 servings

 If you don't have enough time to make the sauce you can use your favorite prepared spaghetti sauce.

Shells:

25 jumbo pasta shells
1½ cups (6 ounces) ricotta cheese
¾ cup (3 ounces) shredded mozzarella cheese
¾ cup (3 ounces) freshly grated Parmesan cheese
½ teaspoon ground white pepper
½ teaspoon paprika
1 tablespoon finely chopped parsley
½ cup chopped green onions
8 ounces lump crabmeat, picked over

Sauce:

3 tablespoons vegetable oil
2 cups finely chopped onion
1 cup finely chopped green bell pepper
½ cup finely chopped red bell pepper
1 tablespoon Enola's Special Seasoning
6 tablespoons tomato paste
1 teaspoon dry basil
3½ cups water, in all

Preheat oven to 400 degrees. Prepare sauce by placing oil in a 5-quart pot over high heat; heat until very hot. Add onion, bell peppers, season-ing, tomato paste and basil. Cook and stir 5 minutes. Add 2 cups of water and cook 10 minutes. Add remaining water and cook an addi-tional 5 minutes. While sauce is cooking, prepare shells according to package directions. Drain and set aside. In a large bowl, combine the 3 cheeses, stirring well. Add white pepper, paprika, parsley and green onion. Fold in crabmeat. With a small spoon, spoon equal amounts of mixture into each pasta shell. Place filled shells in a baking dish. Spoon sauce over shells. Bake 30 minutes or until cheese is melted.

Chef Enola Prudhomme

Donald's Eggplant Pirogue

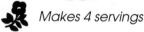 *Makes 4 servings*

2	(1 pound) eggplants
4	tablespoons Enola's Special Seasoning, in all
2	cups all-purpose flour
2	eggs, beaten
1	cup milk
1	cup plain dry bread crumbs
	Vegetable oil
1	dozen shrimp (30 to 35 count), peeled and deveined
2	tablespoons unsalted butter

½	pound small shrimp
⅓	cup finely chopped tasso
1	cup thinly sliced mushrooms
1	cup very finely chopped onion
½	pound Louisiana fresh crawfish tails
½	cup chopped green onion
1½	cup heavy whipping cream
1	cup lump crabmeat, picked over

Peel eggplants and cut in halves lengthwise. Carve each eggplant half into the shape of a boat, tapered at both ends. Scoop out center and reserve pulp. Chop pulp into small cubes and set aside. Season the eggplant boats with 2 tablespoons seasoning. Place flour in a medium bowl. In a medium bowl, combine eggs and milk, stirring well. Dip eggplant in flour, then in egg mixture and then in bread crumbs. Heat oil to 375 degrees. Add eggplant boats, 1 at the time. Cook 8 to 10 minutes or until golden brown. Drain upside down on paper towel and keep warm. Season 12 shrimp with 1 tablespoon seasoning. Dip in flour, then in egg wash and back in the flour. Fry 10 minutes or until golden brown. Place on paper towel and keep warm. In a medium skillet over high heat, melt butter and add shrimp, tasso and reserved eggplant cubes. Cook and stir 5 minutes. Add mushrooms, onion, crawfish and green onion. Cook 5 minutes. Add cream and crabmeat. Cook an additional 10 minutes or until sauce is thickened. Place each eggplant pirogue on a plate and spoon shrimp mixture evenly among pirogues. Place 3 fried shrimp on top of each.

Chef Donald Hebert

Shrimp Pasta

 Makes 4 servings

1	(16 ounce) package rotini pasta	⅓	cup shrimp stock or water
¼	cup butter or margarine	½	cup chopped green onion tops
1	pound medium shrimp, peeled and deveined	¾	cup thinly sliced fresh mushrooms
2	teaspoons seafood seasoning, in all	2	cups heavy whipping cream

Cook rotini according to package directions and set aside. In 5-quart pot over high heat, melt butter. Add shrimp and 1 teaspoon seasoning. Cook and stir 2 minutes. Stir in the stock or water and cook 7 minutes. Add the onion tops, mushrooms, remaining 1 teaspoon seasoning, and cream. Cook over medium heat 6 to 8 minutes. Add pasta to mixture and reduce heat to low. Cook 3 additional minutes.

Chef Donald Hebert

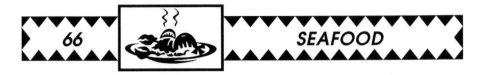

Shrimp or Crawfish Rice Casserole

 *Makes 6 servings*

¼	cup butter or margarine	1	(10¾ ounce) canned
1	cup chopped onion		condensed cream of celery
½	cup chopped red bell		soup, undiluted
	pepper	1	(10¾ ounce) canned
½	cup chopped green bell		condensed cream of
	pepper		mushroom soup, undiluted
2	stalks finely chopped celery	1	cup raw converted rice
1	pound small shrimp or	¼	cup chopped green onion
	crawfish tails	3	tablespoons very finely
			chopped parsley

Preheat oven to 375 degrees. In a medium skillet over high heat, melt butter. Add onion, bell pepper, celery and shrimp or crawfish. Cook and stir 3 minutes or until vegetables are transparent and shellfish are pink. Add celery soup and mushroom soup, stirring well. Add rice, green onion and parsley. Cook 2 to 3 minutes until well mixed. Spray 12x9x2-inch baking dish with vegetable cooking spray. Spoon mixture into dish and cover. Bake 45 minutes. Uncover several times while baking to stir well and check rice. Depending on the rice used, it may need a little less or more time to become tender. For best results use converted rice.

Chef Enola Prudhomme

Louisiana Crawfish Ettouffe

 Makes 4 to 6 servings

3	tablespoons unsalted butter or margarine	1	(10¾ ounce) can cream of mushroom soup, undiluted
3	tablespoons all-purpose flour	2	teaspoons salt
1	cup finely chopped onion	½	teaspoon ground black pepper
½	cup finely chopped celery	¼	teaspoon ground red pepper
½	cup finely chopped bell pepper	1	pound Louisiana crawfish tails
3	tablespoons tomato paste	½	cup finely chopped green onion
3	cups seafood stock, beef broth or water	¼	cup finely chopped parsley

In a 5-quart pot over high heat, melt butter. Add flour, stirring constantly to make a roux. When mixture becomes brownish red in color, add onion, celery and bell pepper. Reduce heat to medium and cook 5 minutes, stirring often. Dissolve tomato paste in the stock, broth or water; add to roux mixture. Cover and cook 15 minutes, stirring occasionally. Add soup, salt, black pepper and red pepper. Cover and cook 15 minutes. Add crawfish tails, green onion and parsley. Cook and stir 10 minutes. Remove from heat, cover and let stand 5 minutes before serving. Serve over rice or fettuccine.

Chef Enola Prudhomme

Grilled Shrimp with Lime Garlic Butter Sauce Over Angel Hair Pasta

 Makes 4 servings

Pasta and Shrimp:

1 (8 ounce) package angel hair pasta

1 pound medium shrimp (30 to 35 count), peeled and deveined

1 tablespoon seafood seasoning

2 tablespoons lime juice

Sauce:

2 tablespoons butter or margarine

2 teaspoons minced garlic

1 cup julienne-cut red bell pepper

1 cup julienne-cut green bell pepper

1 cup medium tomatoes peeled, seeded and finely chopped

2 teaspoons seafood seasoning

¼ cup finely chopped green onion

½ cup water

3 tablespoons dry vermouth (optional)

Pasta and Shrimp:
In a medium bowl, combine shrimp, seafood seasoning and lime juice. Stir well to mix. Marinate overnight. Cook pasta according to package directions, rinse and set aside. Keep warm. Thread shrimp on skewer and place on hot grill. Baste shrimp with marinate 2 to 3 times while grilling. Grill 3 minutes on each side or until shrimp are done. Remove from skewers, set aside and keep warm.

Sauce:
In a medium skillet over high heat, melt butter. Combine garlic, bell pepper and tomatoes. Cook and stir 3 minutes. Add seafood seasoning, green onion, water and vermouth. Cook and stir 3 minutes. Pour sauce over pasta and top with shrimp. Serve immediately.

Chef Enola Prudhomme

C.J.O. Crab Cakes

 Makes 4 (8 ounce) servings

½ cup butter or margarine	1½ tablespoons paprika
½ cup finely chopped celery	2 tablespoons finely chopped parsley
2 cups finely chopped onion	
1 cup finely chopped red bell pepper	1 egg, beaten
1 cup finely chopped green bell pepper	1½ cups dry bread crumbs
	2 cups claw crabmeat, picked over
1½ teaspoons salt	2 tablespoons chopped green onion
1½ tablespoons ground white pepper	½ cup heavy whipping cream

In a 5-quart pot over high heat, combine butter, celery, onion, bell pepper, salt, white pepper, paprika and parsley. Cook 10 minutes or until vegetables are tender. Remove from heat. Pour cooked mixture into a food processor. Press pulse button 3 or 4 times. In a medium bowl, combine processed mixture, egg and bread crumbs, stirring to mix well. Add crabmeat, green onion and cream. Mix well. Form into 4 patties. Heat grill or griddle until very hot. Spray both side of patties with vegetable cooking spray to prevent sticking. Cook 2 to 3 minutes on each side. Serve hot.

Chef Chris Oncale

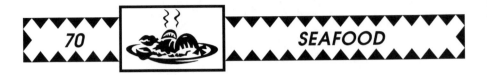

Shrimp Fettuccine Rouge

Makes 4 servings

1 (16 ounce) package fettuccine	1 pound medium shrimp, peeled and deveined
¼ cup butter or margarine	¼ cup shrimp stock or water
½ cup finely chopped onion	2 (8 ounce) cans tomato sauce
¼ cup finely chopped green bell pepper	1 (6 ounce) can tomato paste
¼ cup finely chopped celery	2 teaspoons sugar
2 teaspoons Enola's Special Seasoning, in all	½ cup chopped green onion tops
	¾ cup sliced mushrooms

Cook pasta according to package directions, rinse and set aside. In a 4-quart sauce pan over medium high heat, melt butter. Add onion, bell pepper, celery and 1 teaspoon seasoning. Cook 8 to 10 minutes, stirring often. Add shrimp and the remaining 1 teaspoon seasoning. Cook 5 minutes. Add stock or water and continue cooking 5 minutes. Add tomato sauce, tomato paste and sugar. Cook and stir for 10 minutes. Add green onion, mushrooms and fettuccine. Cook an additional 5 minutes. Serve hot.

Chef Donald Hebert

Hot Shrimp Rice

 Makes 4 servings

2 tablespoons butter or margarine
2 cups finely chopped onion
¼ cup finely chopped green bell pepper
½ cup finely chopped red bell pepper
1½ cups small shrimp (about 1 pound), peeled and deveined

½ cup water
2 (10¾ ounce) cans cream of mushroom soup, undiluted
1 teaspoon salt
¼ teaspoon ground red pepper
½ teaspoon chopped parsley
½ cup finely chopped green onion
3 cups cooked rice

In a 8-quart pot over medium heat, melt butter. Add the onion and bell pepper. Cook and stir 8 minutes or until vegetables are tender. Add shrimp. Cook and stir 3 minutes or until shrimp turn pink. Add water and mushroom soup. Cook and stir 8 minutes over medium heat. Add salt, red pepper, parsley and green onion. Cook 5 additional minutes. Stir in rice and mix well.

Chef Sonny Aymond

Shrimp Rémoulade

Makes 6 servings

 This dish is guaranteed to be a great hit at any party!

½ cup mildly hot and sweet sauce	1½ cups finely chopped green onion
½ cup olive oil	2 cups mayonnaise
1 large green bell pepper, seeded	3 tablespoons vinegar
½ cup parsley tops	1 tablespoon paprika
¼ cup horseradish	4 jalapeño peppers, seeded
1 cup brown mustard	2½ cups water
2 tablespoons ground black pepper	1 tablespoon salt
2 cups finely chopped onion	1½ teaspoons ground red pepper
1 cup ketchup	36 large shrimp (30 to 35 count), peeled and deveined

In food processor, combine hot and sweet sauce, oil, bell pepper, parsley, horseradish, mustard, black pepper, onion, ketchup, green onion, mayonnaise, vinegar, paprika and jalapeño peppers. Process until well chopped. Pour mixture into a bowl and set aside. In a 5-quart pot over high heat, combine water, salt and red pepper. Bring to a boil. Add shrimp and cook 10 minutes or until shrimp turn pink. When shrimp are cooked, remove from heat. Drain, place in ice water and let stand 10 minutes. Drain shrimp and add to the sauce. Place shrimp in refrigerator and marinate 4 hours. Serve in individual cocktail dishes or on a party tray.

Chef Sonny Aymond

Hot and Sweet Shrimp Pasta

 Makes 4 servings

2 tablespoons butter or margarine	1 cup thinly sliced fresh mushrooms
1 pound shrimp (30 to 35), peeled and deveined	2 cups heavy whipping cream
3 tablespoons hot and sweet pizza and pasta seasoning, in all	3 cups cooked pasta
	1 teaspoon minced garlic
½ teaspoon salt	½ cup finely chopped green onion
1 cup very finely chopped onion	½ cup (2 ounces) shredded Cheddar cheese
	½ cup (2 ounces) shredded Monterey Jack cheese

In a medium skillet over high heat, heat butter until very hot. Add shrimp and 2 tablespoons seasoning, salt, onion and mushrooms. Cook and stir 10 minutes. Add cream, pasta and garlic. Cook and stir 5 minutes or until sauce is thickened. Add green onion and both cheeses. Cook and stir 3 minutes. Add remaining 1 tablespoon seasoning and cook 1 minute. Serve hot.

Chef Enola Prudhomme

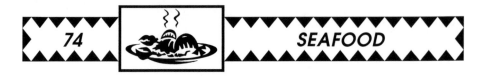

Crawfish or Shrimp Cajun Enchilada

 Makes 12 servings

¼ cup plus 2 tablespoons butter or margarine, in all
2 cups chopped onion
1 cup chopped red bell pepper
2 (8 ounce) packages cream cheese
1 cup sour cream
2½ teaspoons oregano leaves
2½ teaspoons ground cumin
2 teaspoons salt
¼ teaspoon ground red pepper

2½ cups heavy whipping cream
3 pounds crawfish or small shrimp tails
4 teaspoons seafood seasoning
½ cup chopped green onion
12 (6 inch) flour tortillas
2 cups (8 ounces) freshly grated Monterey Jack cheese
Parsley sprigs for garnish

In a 5-quart pot over high heat, melt ¼ cup butter or margarine. Add onion and bell pepper. Cook and stir 5 minutes. Reduce heat to medium and cook an additional 5 minutes. Add cream cheese, sour cream, oregano, cumin, salt and red pepper. Cook and stir 3 minutes. Add whipping cream and cook 5 minutes. In a medium skillet over high heat, combine remaining 2 tablespoons butter or margarine and crawfish or shrimp. Cook and stir 3 minutes. Add seasoning and green onion. Cook an additional 2 minutes. Add to cream mixture and mix well. Spoon portion of shellfish mixture in the center of each tortilla. Fold the tortilla in thirds and place seam side down. Spoon remaining mixture over the tortilla and top with cheese. Garnish with a parsley sprig.

Chef Enola Prudhomme

Baked or Fried Stuffed Crabs

 *Makes 12*

½ cup butter or margarine
3 cups finely chopped onion
½ cup finely chopped green bell pepper
½ cup finely chopped red bell pepper
1 teaspoon salt
½ teaspoon ground red pepper
1 tablespoon Worcestershire sauce

⅛ teaspoon garlic powder
2 eggs
½ cup heavy whipping cream
1 tablespoon lemon juice
1¼ cups fine dry bread crumbs, in all
1 pound lump or claw crabmeat, picked over
¼ teaspoon paprika

In a heavy skillet over high heat, melt butter. Add onion and green bell pepper. Cook and stir 10 minutes. Add bell pepper, salt, red pepper, Worcestershire sauce and garlic powder. Cook and stir 10 minutes. In a small bowl, beat eggs in cream and set aside. Remove vegetable sauce from heat and let cool 5 minutes; it should be warm but not hot. Slowly stir in the egg and cream mixture. Add lemon juice and 1 cup bread crumbs. Fold in crabmeat, being careful not to break it up. Fill crab shell (foil shell works well) and chill 2 hours. Preheat oven to 375 degrees. Sprinkle remaining ¼ cup bread crumbs and paprika over crabs before baking. Bake 20 minutes or until the top is golden brown.

Fried Stuffed Crabs:

2 eggs
1 (16-ounce) can evaporated milk
½ cup water

1½ cups fine dry bread crumbs
1½ cups all-purpose flour
2 cups vegetable oil

In a medium bowl, beat eggs with milk and water. Set aside. Sprinkle bread crumbs over crabs, dredge in flour, dip in egg wash, then again in flour, egg wash and bread crumbs. Fry crabs in hot oil 5 minutes or until golden brown. For best results, refrigerate for 2 to 3 hours before frying.

Chef Enola Prudhomme

Sensational Garlic Shrimp

 *Makes 4 servings*

1	tablespoon butter or margarine	¼	cup white wine or water
1	tablespoon olive oil	½	cup heavy whipping cream
24	medium shrimp, peeled, deveined	2	teaspoons minced garlic
1	tablespoon plus 2 teaspoons seafood magic	¼	cup (1 ounce) freshly grated Parmesan cheese
			Hot cooked pasta

In a medium skillet over high heat, combine butter and oil. Add shrimp and seasoning. Cook and stir 5 minutes. Add wine, bring to a boil and cook and stir 3 minutes. Remove shrimp, place on plate and keep warm. To skillet, add cream, garlic and cheese. Cook and stir 3 minutes. Return shrimp to skillet and cook an additional 3 minutes or until sauce thickens. Serve over pasta.

Chef Enola Prudhomme

Sautéed Sea Scallops with Lemon Garlic Sauce

 Makes 4 servings

6 tablespoons butter or margarine, in all	½ cup champagne
½ medium-sized onion, thinly sliced	1 tablespoon minced garlic
	1½ teaspoons grated fresh ginger
½ medium-sized green bell pepper, cut julienne	½ teaspoon salt
	¼ teaspoon ground red pepper
½ medium-sized red bell pepper, cut julienne	1 pound sea scallops
2 tablespoons fresh lemon juice	½ cup heavy whipping cream
	2 cups cooked pasta
	¼ cup chopped green onion

In a medium skillet over high heat, melt 4 tablespoons butter or margarine. Add onion and bell pepper. Cook and stir 3 minutes. Add lemon juice, champagne, garlic, ginger, salt, red pepper and scallops. Cook and stir 5 minutes. Remove from heat, place scallops on platter and keep warm. In the same skillet over high heat, combine remaining 2 tablespoons butter or margarine and whipping cream. Bring to boil and cook and stir 4 to 5 minutes. Add cooked pasta and green onion. Return scallops to skillet, stir well and cook an additional 2 to 3 minutes. Serve hot.

Chef Enola Prudhomme

Stuffed Manicotti

Makes 4 to 5 servings

 You will notice I say 4 to 5 servings. I assure you, if your guests are like my staff, it will be 4 servings!

Manicotti:

1½ cups water	½ pound medium shrimp, peeled, deveined and chopped
1 teaspoon salt	
1 teaspoon ground red pepper	
14 manicotti shells	1 pound spinach, torn into small pieces

Filling:

1 (6 ounce) package cream cheese	2½ teaspoons seafood seasoning
¾ cup ricotta cheese	½ cup chopped green onion
¾ cup (3 ounces) Parmesan cheese	

Sauce:

2 tablespoons vegetable oil	½ teaspoon dry Italian seasoning
1 cup finely chopped onion	
½ cup finely chopped green bell pepper	2½ cups water
	½ teaspoon salt
1 (6-ounce) can tomato paste	½ cup ricotta cheese

Manicotti:

In a 5-quart pot, bring water to a boil. Add salt, pepper and manicotti pasta. Cook 5 minutes. With a slotted spoon, remove pasta and set aside. In the same liquid, add shrimp and cook 5 minutes. Remove shrimp and set aside. Using the same liquid, bring to a boil and add spinach. Cook, stirring occasionally, 5 minutes. Drain and discard liquid. Divide spinach in half and set aside.

(Stuffed Manicotti continued on next page)

(Stuffed Manicotti continued)

Filling:
In a medium bowl, combine cream cheese and ricotta cheese, stirring until smooth. Add Parmesan cheese, seasoning, green onion, half of cooked spinach and all of shrimp. Fill each manicotti with equal amounts of mixture. Place manicotti in a 13x9x2-inch oiled pan in a single layer.

Sauce:
In a medium skillet over high heat, combine oil, onions, bell pepper, tomato paste and seasoning. Cook 2 to 3 minutes. Add water and salt. Cook and stir 5 to 6 minutes or until onions are tender. Add remaining spinach and ricotta cheese. Cook and stir 10 minutes longer. With a large pastry bag and a large tip (#805), fill the bag with mixture. Spoon sauce over each manicotti. Cover with foil. Bake at 350 degrees for 20 minutes. Serve hot.

Chef Enola Prudhomme

Andouille and Crawfish Fettuccine

Makes 4 servings

 If crawfish are not available, you can substitute fresh shrimp or sea scallops.

2	tablespoons butter or margarine	½	cup thinly sliced fresh mushrooms
½	pound andouille sausage, cut in ½-inch pieces	4	cups cooked fettuccine
1	pound peeled Louisiana crawfish tails, deveined	4	cups heavy whipping cream
		2	teaspoons seafood seasoning
½	cup seafood stock or water	¼	cup finely chopped green onion

Melt the butter in a large skillet over high heat. Add andouille and cook and stir 2 minutes. Add the crawfish, stock, and mushrooms. Cook and stir 3 minutes. Add fettuccine and cook 2 minutes, stirring often to prevent sticking. Add cream, seasoning and green onion. Cook and stir 10 minutes or until sauce thickens.

Chef Chris Oncale

FISH

Marinated Salmon Steak

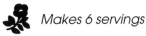 *Makes 6 servings*

4 tablespoons olive oil	½ cup white wine
½ teaspoon grated lemon peel	½ teaspoon salt
1½ tablespoons minced garlic	⅛ teaspoon ground red pepper
1 teaspoon tarragon	6 salmon steaks, ½-inch thick
1 teaspoon whole basil	

In medium bowl, mix oil, lemon, garlic, tarragon, basil, wine, salt and red pepper. Lay salmon steaks in 2-inch deep baking pan. Pour mixture evenly over salmon. Place in refrigerator for 3 hours, turning every half hour. Remove salmon from marinade. Place on hot grill or broil for 3 to 5 minutes on each side.

Chef Sonny Aymond

Catfish Courtbouillon

 *Makes 4 servings*

2 tablespoons butter or margarine	½ teaspoon ground red pepper
3 cups coarsely chopped onion	2 cups water or stock
1 cup coarsely chopped green bell pepper	1 (8 ounce) can tomato sauce
1 tablespoon minced garlic	2 tablespoons roux
½ cup finely chopped celery	4 (7 to 9 ounce) catfish fillets
2 tablespoons seafood seasoning	½ teaspoon sugar
	1 cup chopped green onion
	1 tablespoon finely chopped parsley

In a 5-quart pot over high heat, melt butter or margarine. Add onion, bell pepper, garlic and celery. Cook and stir for 15 minutes. Add seafood seasoning, red pepper, water or stock, tomato sauce and roux. Reduce heat to medium and cook 5 minutes, stirring occasionally. Reduce heat to simmer and cook 20 minutes, stirring occasionally. Add fish, sugar, green onion and parsley. Cover and cook 15 minutes, stirring occasionally. Remove from heat and let stand a few minutes to allow the flavors to marry before serving.

Chef Sonny Aymond

Pan-Fried Catfish
with Marsala Cream Sauce

 *Makes 4 servings*

Fish:

4	(6 or 7 ounce) catfish filets
3	tablespoons plus ½ teaspoon seafood seasoning, in all
1	egg
1	cup milk
1	cup all-purpose flour
1	cup vegetable oil

Sauce:

2	tablespoons unsalted butter or margarine
2	cups julienne-cut onion
2	cups julienne-cut green bell pepper
2	cups julienne-cut red bell pepper
½	cup peeled, seeded and chopped tomato
3	tablespoons Marsala wine
½	teaspoon seafood seasoning
1	cup heavy whipping cream
¼	cup chopped green onion

Fish:
Place filets on a clean, flat surface. Sprinkle 2 tablespoons seasoning over both sides of filets and set aside. In a small bowl, beat together egg and milk and set aside. Add the remaining seasoning to the flour and stir well. Dredge filets through flour, dip in egg and then in flour. Heat oil in a large skillet over high heat. Place filets in oil and cook 3 minutes on each side or until golden brown. Drain filets on paper towel.

Sauce:
In a medium skillet over high heat, melt butter or margarine. Add onion, bell pepper, tomato, wine and seasoning. Cook and stir 3 minutes. Reduce heat to medium and stir in cream. Cook and stir 5 minutes or until sauce thickens. Add green onion and cook additional 1 minute. Spoon sauce over catfish filets and serve hot. Serve immediately.

Chef Enola Prudhomme

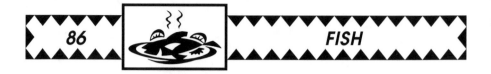
Seafood Eggplant Casserole Oncale

 Makes 6 servings

¼	cup butter or margarine
¾	cup finely chopped onion
⅓	cup finely chopped green bell pepper
¼	cup finely chopped red bell pepper
2	stalks very finely chopped celery
⅓	cup chopped green onion bottoms
3	pounds fresh eggplant, peeled and cut in 1-inch cubes
4	teaspoons salt
1	tablespoon ground red pepper
½	pound fresh small shrimp, peeled
1	pound fresh lump crabmeat, picked over
1	(6 ounce) catfish filet, cut in bite size pieces
1	cup heavy whipping cream
2½	cups fine dry bread crumbs, in all

Preheat oven to 350 degrees. In a large pot over high heat, combine margarine, onion, bell pepper, celery and green onion bottoms. Sauté 7 minutes, stirring constantly. Add eggplant. Cook and stir 5 minutes. Add salt, red pepper, shrimp, crabmeat and catfish. Cook and stir 4 minutes. Add cream and 2 cups bread crumbs, mixing well. Cook 2 minutes or until mixture thickens. Place in casserole dish. Sprinkle the remaining bread crumbs on top. Bake 25 minutes.

Chef Chris Oncale

Uncle Ralph's Fried Fish

 *Makes 4 servings*

1	teaspoon salt	3	heaping tablespoons
¾	teaspoon ground red pepper		prepared mustard
¾	teaspoon ground black	1	box fish fry
	pepper	2	cups vegetable oil
4	(7 to 9 ounce) fish filets		

In a small bowl, combine salt, red pepper and black pepper, mixing well. Sprinkle over both sides of each filet. Rub mustard over both sides of filets. Place the fish fry in a flat plate and dredge each filet in fish fry until well coated. In a large skillet, heat oil until very hot. Carefully place each filet in skillet, making sure the filets do not touch. Cook 3 to 5 minutes or until golden brown. Remove from hot oil using a slotted spatula and place on paper towel to drain. Serve with French fries and green salad.

Chef Enola Prudhomme

Stuffed Red Snapper with Shrimp and Crabmeat Cream Sauce

Makes 4 servings

 This recipe was one of my first silver medal winners!

Fish:

1½	pounds red snapper filets	1	cup finely chopped onion
1	tablespoon salt	¼	cup finely chopped green bell pepper
1	tablespoon onion powder	¼	cup finely chopped red bell pepper
1	tablespoon garlic powder		
1	tablespoon ground white pepper	¼	cup finely chopped celery
1	tablespoon oregano	½	pound small shrimp, peeled
1	tablespoon sweet basil	1	cup heavy whipping cream
2	teaspoons ground red pepper	1	cup fine dry bread crumbs
3	tablespoons butter or margarine	½	pound fresh lump crabmeat, picked over

Cream Sauce:

3	tablespoons butter or margarine, in all	¼	cup finely chopped green onions
½	pound small shrimp, peeled	2	teaspoons reserved seasoning mix
1	cup fresh mushrooms, thinly sliced	1	cup heavy whipping cream

Fish:

Preheat oven to 375 degrees. Cut each filet in half lengthwise, being careful not to cut all the way through, forming a pocket. In a small bowl, combine salt, onion powder, garlic powder, white pepper, oregano, basil and red pepper. Mix well, and sprinkle 1½ tablespoons over both sides of fish and inside cavity. Set filets aside. In a medium skillet over high heat, melt butter or margarine. Add the onion, bell pepper, celery and 1 tablespoon seasoning mixture. Cook and stir 5 minutes. Add shrimp and cook 5 minutes, stirring constantly. Stir in cream and cook 5 minutes. Remove from heat and carefully fold in bread crumbs and crabmeat. Set aside and let cool to touch. Place seasoned filets on a clean flat surface. Spoon equal portions of stuffing mixture into cavity of each filet. Close cavities and place filets on a baking sheet sprayed with vegetable cooking spray. Place under broiler, about 7 inches from heat. Broil 10 to

(Stuffed Red Snapper continued on next page)

(Stuffed Red Snapper continued)

12 minutes or until fish flakes easily with a fork. While fish is broiling, prepare cream sauce. Remove filets from broiler. Place each on a plate and spoon equal portions of the cream sauce over each one. Serve hot.

Cream Sauce:
In a medium skillet over high heat, melt 2 tablespoons butter or margarine. Add shrimp, mushrooms, green onion and seasoning. Cook, stirring constantly. When shrimp begin to stick to skillet, add the cream.

Cook and stir 5 minutes. Add the remaining 1 tablespoon butter or margarine and cook 3 to 4 minutes or until thickened.

Chef Enola Prudhomme

Stuffed Catfish with Crawfish and Crabmeat Cream Sauce

Makes 4 servings

 First Gold Medal winner at Baton Rouge Culinary Classes.

Fish and Stuffing:

4   (6 ounce) catfish filets
3   tablespoons plus ½ teaspoon seafood seasoning, in all
5   tablespoon butter or margarine, in all
1   cup finely chopped onion
½   cup finely chopped red bell pepper
½   cup finely chopped green bell pepper

½   cup seafood stock
½   cup beef broth or stock
¼   cup chopped green onion
1   cup heavy whipping cream
2½   cups toasted bread, (about 4 slices), cubed
½   pound lump crabmeat, picked over
¼   pound chopped crawfish tails

Sauce:

2   tablespoons butter or margarine
1   cup (about ½ pound) Louisiana crawfish tails
1   cup thinly sliced mushrooms

4   teaspoons seafood seasoning
½   pound lump crabmeat, picked over
¼   cup sliced green onion
1   cup heavy whipping cream

Fish and Stuffing:
Place filets on cutting board. Cut each filet in half lengthwise, being careful not to cut through, forming a pocket. Sprinkle 2½ teaspoons seasoning evenly over fish and inside cavity and set aside. In a medium skillet over medium heat, melt 3 tablespoons butter or margarine. Add onion, bell pepper and 2 teaspoons seasoning. Cook and stir 5 minutes. Add broth or stock and green onion. Cook and stir 3 minutes. Add cream. Cook and stir 5 minutes or until sauce reduces and begins to thickens. Add bread, remove from heat and stir well. Carefully fold in crabmeat and set aside to cool. Spray baking sheet with vegetable cooking spray. Place the filets on the baking sheet. Divide stuffing into four equal portions, place inside each filet and close. Spray tops of filets with vegetable spray. Broil about 6 or 7 inches from flame for 10 minutes or until fish is done. Place fish on a larger platter and keep warm.

(Stuffed Catfish continued on next page)

(Stuffed Catfish continued)

For Sauce:
In a medium skillet, melt butter or margarine over high heat. Add crawfish, mushroom and seasoning. Cook and stir 3 minutes. Add crabmeat and green onion. Cook 3 minutes. Being careful not to break up crabmeat, add cream. Cook and stir 5 minutes or until cream is thickened. Place fish on plates and spoon sauce over fish. Makes 2 cups

Chef Enola Prudhomme

Enola's Catfish Over Seafood Stuffing

 *Makes 4 servings*

Fish and Stuffing:

5	(7 to 8 ounce) catfish filets
3	tablespoons plus
	2 teaspoons Enola's Special
	seasoning, in all
2	cups water
½	pound small shrimp, peeled
	and deveined
¼	cup butter or margarine
2	cups finely chopped onion
¼	cup finely chopped green
	bell pepper
1	teaspoon salt
1	teaspoon browning sauce
½	cup heavy whipping cream
1	cup fine dry bread crumbs
1	pound fresh lump crabmeat,
	picked over

Batter:

2	eggs
2	cups evaporated milk
2	cups all-purpose flour
4	cups vegetable oil

Cheese Sauce:

2	tablespoons butter or
	margarine
1	tablespoon all-purpose flour
1	cup heavy whipping cream
1	cup (4 ounces) shredded
	Cheddar cheese
½	teaspoon ground white
	pepper

Fish and Stuffing:

Cut one filet in small cubes and set aside for stuffing. Season 4 fillets on both sides with 2 tablespoons Enola's seasoning and set aside. In a 5-quart pot over high heat, combine water, 2 teaspoons seasoning, cubed fillet and shrimp. Bring to a boil and cook and stir 5 minutes or until fish is done. With a slotted spoon, remove fish and shrimp. Reserving 1 cup liquid, discard remaining liquid. In the same pot over high heat, melt butter or margarine. Add onion and bell pepper. Cook and stir 10 minutes. Add salt, then reduce heat to medium. Add fish, shrimp, 1 tablespoon seasoning and reserved liquid. Cook and stir 10 minutes. Add browning sauce and cream. Cook 5 minutes, stirring occasionally. Remove from heat. Add bread crumbs and fold in crabmeat, mixing well. Set aside.

(Catfish Over Seafood Stuffing continued on next page)

(Catfish Over Seafood Stuffing continued)

Batter:
Beat eggs with milk until well mixed. Dredge seasoned fish fillets in flour, dip in egg mixture, then dredge again in flour. In a large skillet, over high heat, heat oil to 350 degrees. Cook each fillet 4 minutes on each side, cooking no more then 2 fillets at a time. Place cooked fillets on paper towel to drain.

Cheese Sauce:
In a medium skillet over low heat, melt butter or margarine. Add flour and cook and stir for a few seconds; be careful not to let flour brown. Add cream, cheese and white pepper. Cook and stir until cheese is melted and thickens.

Assemble:
Place equal amount of stuffing on each of four plates. Place fish fillets over stuffing. Drizzle cheese sauce over top of each fillet. Serve hot with a side dish of steamed broccoli and cauliflower.

Chef Enola Prudhomme

Marinated Grilled Fish with Horseradish

 Makes 4 servings

1½	pounds tilapia or favorite fish	3	tablespoons horseradish
3½	tablespoons seafood seasoning, in all	1	tablespoon fresh lemon juice
		½	cup heavy whipping cream
2	tablespoons butter or margarine	½	cup finely chopped green onion
6	ounces small shrimp, peeled and deveined	1	tablespoon parsley

Season fish with 1 tablespoon plus 1 teaspoon seafood seasoning. Cover and let marinate for at least 2 hours. Heat grill until very hot. Spray both sides of fish with cooking spray. Place fish on grill and cook 4 minutes, carefully turn fish over and cook additional 5 minutes. Place on large platter and keeping hot. In a medium skillet over high heat, melt butter and heat until very hot. Add shrimp, horseradish, lemon juice, cream, green onion, parsley and remaining seafood seasoning. Cook and stir 5 minutes or until sauce thickens. Place each fish on a plate and spoon equal amount of sauce over each filet.

Chef Enola Prudhomme

Parmesan Baked Tilapia

Makes 4 servings

 Tilapia, a firm white flesh fish, is farmed in ponds in Louisiana. If you can't find it, you can substitute snapper or orange roughy.

4	(6 ounce) fresh tilapia filets	3	tablespoons finely chopped green onion
½	cup mayonnaise		
¼	cup (1 ounce) grated Parmesan cheese	1	teaspoon Worcestershire sauce

Preheat oven to 400 degrees. Rinse fish and pat dry with paper towels. Spray a 13x9x2-inch baking dish with nonstick cooking spray. Place filets in dish and set aside. In a small bowl, combine mayonnaise, cheese, green onion and Worcestershire sauce, mixing well. Spread over fish filets. Bake, uncovered, 20 minutes or until fish flakes easily when tested with a fork.

Chef Chris Oncale

Smoked Catfish

Makes 6 servings

 Combine the recipe for Chris's Fresh Spinach with the Smoked Catfish and top it with your favorite sauce. Great!

6	(5 to 6 ounce) catfish filets	½	teaspoon hickory smoke seasoning
2	teaspoons Enola's Special seasoning		

Place filets on a cutting board. Sprinkle both seasonings evenly over both sides of filets. In a smoker or a barbecue pit, place fish on top rack. Cook 15 minutes on both sides.

Chef Chris Oncale

Judy's Baked Fish

 *Makes 4 servings*

2 tablespoons butter or margarine, in all	1 tablespoon grated lemon peel
¼ cup very finely chopped onion	1 teaspoon salt
¼ cup very finely chopped parsley	¼ teaspoon ground red pepper
¼ cup plain dry bread crumbs	¼ teaspoon ground white pepper
	1 tablespoon Dijon mustard
	4 (7 to 9 ounce) catfish filets

Preheat oven to 400 degrees. Spread a 13x9x2-inch baking pan with 1 teaspoon butter or margarine. In a medium bowl, combine onion, parsley, bread crumbs, lemon peel, salt, red pepper and white pepper, mixing well. Rub the mustard on both sides of each fillet, using fingertips. Place fish on platter and sprinkle bread crumb mixture over both sides of each fillet. Place fish in baking pan and dot with remaining butter. Bake, uncovered, for 30 minutes.

Chef Enola Prudhomme

Beau's Baked Catfish

Makes 4 servings

 Last year my son Beau lost 30 pounds! He loves this baked fish with green beans and salad. This hearty meal gives him the energy he needs to play on the baseball team at school. (It also keeps him slim for all those school girls!)

1	tablespoon butter or margarine, melted	1	tablespoon Worcestershire sauce
1	tablespoon salt	1	tablespoon bottled Italian dressing
1½	teaspoons ground black pepper	1	small red onion, thinly sliced
4	(6 to 8 ounce) fresh catfish filets	½	small green bell pepper, cut julienne
2	tablespoons fresh lemon juice		

Preheat oven to 350 degrees. Spread butter or margarine in a 9x6x2-inch baking dish. Sprinkle salt and black pepper over both sides of filets and place in baking dish. In a small bowl, combine lemon juice, Worcestershire sauce and Italian dressing. Drizzle over fish. Arrange onion and bell pepper on top. Cover with foil and bake 20 minutes; uncover and bake additional 15 minutes.

Chef Sonny Aymond

Enola's Catfish in Red Gravy

Makes 6 servings

3	pounds fresh catfish filets	1	cup finely chopped green bell pepper
1	teaspoon salt		
1	teaspoon ground red pepper	1	cup ketchup
1	teaspoon ground black pepper	3	tablespoons all-purpose flour
		½	cup water
3	tablespoons unsalted butter	½	cup finely chopped green onion tops
1	cup finely chopped onion		
1	cup finely chopped celery		

Cut filets into ¾-inch thick pieces. Sprinkle salt, red pepper and black pepper over both sides of the fish and set aside. In a large heavy skillet over medium heat, melt butter. Add the onion, celery and bell pepper. Cook and stir 5 minutes or until onions are transparent. Add the ketchup, reduce heat to simmer, cover and cook 15 to 18 minutes. Dissolve the flour in water and add to the skillet along with the fish. Add the onion tops and cook 10 to 12 minutes or until fish is tender, stirring occasionally to prevent from sticking.

Chef Enola Prudhomme

Poached Salmon with Zucchini

 *Makes 4 servings*

1½ pounds medium size zucchini	1 medium-sized onion, thinly sliced
4 (6 ounce) salmon fillets	1 medium-sized green bell pepper, thinly sliced
1½ teaspoon salt, in all	½ cup water
½ teaspoon ground black pepper	2 tablespoons butter or margarine

Cut 5 ounces of zucchini in paper thin rounds. Place in overlapping pattern over salmon. Top with onions and bell pepper. Sprinkle with 1 teaspoon salt and black pepper. Wrap each piece tightly with plastic wrap and refrigerate 30 minutes. Cut remaining zucchini in halves lengthwise, then cut lengths into ½-inch pieces. Add to medium sized pot with water and remaining ½ teaspoon salt. Bring to boil, reduce heat, cover and cook 15 minutes. Unwrap salmon. Place in 1 inch of water in large shallow pan. Place pan over medium heat and cook until tiny bubbles form around edge of pan. Reduce heat so water no longer bubbles and continue cooking until filets are thoroughly cooked. Water temperature should be between 160 and 180 degrees. Transfer half of cooked zucchini and half of mixture into a blender and puree until smooth. Set aside. Transfer remaining zucchini and mixture into a blender and puree until smooth. Add butter and puree until creamy. To serve, place ¼ cup of dark sauce on plate, top with salmon filet and 2 tablespoons buttery sauce. Serve hot.

Chef Donald Hebert

Baked Amberjack

Makes 4 servings

 This recipe is so easy to make! While it is in the oven, I can do the laundry or drive the kids to ball practice. Your family will think you spent hours preparing it!

2	pounds amberjack fish or any firm flesh fish	1½	ounces thinly sliced green bell pepper
1	tablespoon plus 1 teaspoon seafood seasoning	1½	ounces thinly sliced red bell pepper
2	tablespoons butter or margarine	¼	cup minced celery
1	small onion, thinly sliced	2	tablespoons fresh lemon juice
		½	cup heavy whipping cream

Preheat oven to 375 degrees. Place fish on a clean cutting board and make sure fish are cut the same thickness (my fish was cut 1½ inches thick). Season both sides of fish with seasoning and set aside. Melt butter or margarine and spread in a 9x9x2-inch baking dish. Add onion, bell pepper and celery. Arrange fish in single layer on vegetables. Add lemon juice. Cover with foil and bake 15 minutes; uncover and cook for additional 10 minutes. Remove fish from oven and place on hot platter to keep warm, reserving cooked vegetable mixture. In a medium skillet over high heat, combine vegetable mixture and cream. Cook and stir 8 minutes or until sauce thickens. Spoon sauce evenly over each fish filet. Serve hot.

Chef Enola Prudhomme

Oceans Best Barbecued Shark

Makes 4 servings

2 pounds fresh shark
1 small onion, thinly sliced
1 medium-sized green bell pepper, thinly sliced
1 medium-sized red bell pepper, thinly sliced
½ cup plus 2 tablespoons mildly hot and sweet sauce
½ cup plus 2 tablespoons Worcestershire sauce
1½ cups white wine
1 tablespoon salt
1 teaspoon ground red pepper
1 tablespoon ground white pepper
1 tablespoon garlic powder
2 tablespoons butter or margarine

Cut shark steaks into serving size pieces of about 8 ounces each. In a medium bowl, combine fish, onion, bell pepper, hot and sweet sauce, Worcestershire sauce, wine, salt, red pepper, white pepper and garlic powder. Mix well. Let marinate for 10 to 15 minutes. Discard the onions and bell peppers, reserving liquid. Spray both sides of fish with vegetable cooking spray. Place fish on heated grill. Grill for 2 minutes on each side. Set fish aside and keep warm. In a heavy skillet, combine the butter and reserved liquid. Cook over high heat until liquid is reduced by half. Spoon sauce over shark. Yum yum!

Chef Chris Oncale

Fish in Cream Sauce Over Pasta

 *Makes 4 servings*

6	tablespoons butter or margarine, in all	1½	teaspoons salt
1	cup finely chopped onion	1	teaspoon ground black pepper
1	cup finely chopped red bell pepper	3	pounds white flesh fish, cubed
1	cup finely chopped celery	3	cups heavy whipping cream
1½	teaspoons ground red pepper		Hot cooked pasta

In a large skillet over high heat, melt 4 tablespoons butter or margarine. Add onion, bell pepper, celery, red pepper, salt and black pepper. Cook and stir 10 minutes. Add fish and cook and stir 20 minutes; fish should resemble crabmeat. Add cream and remaining 2 tablespoons butter or margarine. Cook an additional 10 minutes or until sauce thickens. Serve over pasta.

Chef Enola Prudhomme

🌺 Notes

CHICKEN

Chicken Enchiladas

Makes 6 servings

1	tablespoon vegetable oil	1	cup finely chopped onion
1½	pound chicken breast, cut julienne	1	teaspoon granulated garlic
2	teaspoons chili powder	1	teaspoon sugar
1	teaspoon salt	½	cup water
½	teaspoon ground white pepper	1	cup heavy whipping cream
½	teaspoon ground red pepper	1	cup (4 ounces) shredded Cheddar cheese
1	cup thinly sliced fresh mushrooms	1	cup (4 ounces) shredded Monterey Jack cheese, for topping
1	(8 ounce) can tomato sauce	6	tortillas

Preheat oven to 400 degrees. Place oil in a 5-quart pot over high heat and heat until very hot. Add chicken and cook 5 minutes. Add chili powder, salt, white pepper, red pepper, mushrooms, tomato sauce, onion, garlic and sugar. Cook and stir for 10 minutes. Add water and cook and stir 5 minutes. Reduce heat to medium. Add cream and cook and stir 3 minutes. Add Cheddar cheese and stir well to mix. When cheese is melted, remove from heat. Place tortillas on a plate, one at a time. Fill the center of each tortilla with ¼ cup of chicken mixture, fold and place seam down in a 12x9x2-inch baking dish. Repeat until all tortillas are filled. Spoon remaining mixture over tortillas and sprinkle Monterey Jack cheese on top. Bake 10 minutes.

Chef Enola Prudhomme

Chicken Casserole

 Makes 6 servings

1	(2½ pound) chicken
10	cups water
1½	cups crushed corn chips, in all
½	cup butter or margarine
⅓	cup finely chopped onion
⅓	cup finely chopped green bell pepper
⅓	cup finely chopped red bell pepper

1	(10¾ ounce) can condensed cream of chicken soup, undiluted
1	(10¾ ounce) can condensed cream of mushroom soup, undiluted
1	tablespoon salt
1	tablespoon very finely chopped jalapeño peppers
½	cup sour cream
1	cup (4 ounces) shredded cheese

Preheat oven to 350 degrees. Place chicken in a large pot and cover with water. Bring to a boil over high heat, reduce heat to medium and cook 30 minutes or until tender. Remove chicken from broth and cool to touch. Remove skin and bones. Cut meat into bite-sized pieces and set aside. Spray baking dish with vegetable cooking spray. Sprinkle 1 cup corn chips in bottom and set aside. In a medium skillet over high heat, melt butter. Add onion and bell pepper. Sauté 10 minutes or until vegetables are tender. Stir in chicken soup, mushroom soup, salt, jalapeño pepper and sour cream. Cook additional 10 minutes. Layer cubed chicken over chips. Pour cooked sauce over chicken. Sprinkle the remaining ½ cup corn chips and the cheese on top. Bake 25 minutes or until cheese is melted.

Chef Chris Oncale

Grilled Chicken Breast with Avocado Sauce

 Makes 4 servings

¼ cup vegetable oil	2 tablespoons unsalted butter
½ cup red wine	½ cup very finely chopped onion
2 tablespoons lemon juice, in all	½ cup very finely chopped celery
1 tablespoon Worcestershire sauce	1 ripe avocado, peeled and finely chopped
½ teaspoon salt	2 teaspoons poultry seasoning
½ teaspoon ground white pepper	½ cup heavy whipping cream
4 (5 ounce) boneless chicken breasts	

In a large bowl, combine oil, wine, 1 tablespoon lemon juice, Worcestershire sauce, salt and white pepper, stirring well. Add the chicken and mix well. Cover and refrigerate at least 3 hours. Drain chicken, reserving ¼ cup of the marinade. Place chicken on a hot grill and cook 5 minutes on each side or until chicken is done. Place on a platter and keep warm. In a medium skillet over high heat, melt butter. Add onion and celery. Cook and stir 5 minutes. Add avocado, reserved marinade, remaining 1 tablespoon lemon juice, poultry seasoning and cream. Cook and stir 2 to 3 minutes or until sauce thickens. To serve, spoon sauce over grilled chicken.

Chef Enola Prudhomme

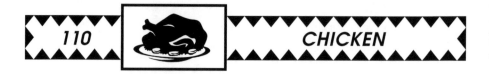
Bronzed Chicken Breast with Honey Orange Sauce

 Makes 4 to 6 servings

1 teaspoon salt	1 tablespoon minced garlic
½ teaspoon ground white pepper	½ cup chopped green bell pepper
½ teaspoon ground red pepper	½ cup chopped red bell pepper
½ teaspoon ground oregano	1 cup orange juice
½ teaspoon basil leaves, crushed	½ cup honey
1 pound boneless, skinless chicken breast	2 tablespoons red wine vinegar
2 tablespoons butter or margarine	1 tablespoon Dijon mustard
1 cup finely chopped onion	1 teaspoon ground ginger

Preheat oven to 475 degrees. In a small bowl, combine salt, white pepper, red pepper, oregano and basil. Sprinkle over both sides of chicken breast and set aside. In a medium skillet over high heat, melt butter or margarine. Add chicken and cook 4 minutes on each side. Remove chicken from the skillet, place in a greased 8x8x2-inch baking dish and set aside. In the same skillet, combine onion, garlic and bell pepper. Cook and stir 5 minutes or until vegetables are tender. Add orange juice, honey, vinegar, mustard and ginger. Cook and stir 6 to 7 minutes or until sauce is reduced by half. Pour over chicken and bake 30 minutes or until tender.

Chef Enola Prudhomme

Tonya's Lemon Pepper Baked Chicken

 *Makes 4 servings*

1	(3 to 4 pound) chicken
3	tablespoons lemon pepper seasoning
2	tablespoons Worcestershire sauce
1	medium-sized onion, quartered
1	medium-sized green bell pepper, quartered
¼	cup chopped green onion
2	teaspoons cornstarch
¼	teaspoon water

Preheat oven to 375 degrees. Wash chicken and cut away all visible fat. Sprinkle lemon pepper and Worcestershire sauce over entire chicken and inside cavity. Place the onion and bell pepper inside cavity. Place chicken in a 6x6x2-inch baking dish. Bake, uncovered, 30 minutes; cover and bake an additional 45 minutes or until chicken is tender and golden brown. Remove chicken from baking dish, place on platter and keep warm. Pour liquid from pan into a skillet. Place over high heat and add green onions. Cook and stir 5 minutes. Dissolve cornstarch in water. Add to skillet, stirring constantly to prevent lumps. Cook and stir an additional 5 minutes. To serve, cut chicken into serving pieces and top with gravy.

Chef Enola Prudhomme

July 4th Neighborhood
Drunken Chicken

Barbecue

 Makes 4 servings

1	(2½ to 2 pound) chicken	1	(12 ounce) can beer
2	tablespoons poultry seasoning	1	cup Italian salad dressing

Wash chicken well. Sprinkle seasoning evenly over chicken. Light barbecue pit coals and when hot, place chicken upright on open can of beer on grate. Close pit. Cook slow for approximately 1 hour or until tender, basting chicken often with Italian dressing. Serve with rice dressing and potato salad.

Chef Sonny Aymond

Cheesy Chicken Rolls

Makes 4 servings

½ cup (2 ounces) shredded Colby-Jack cheese blend	4 skinless and boneless medium chicken breast halves
2½ ounces fresh sliced mushrooms	½ teaspoon salt
¼ cup plain yogurt plus 1 tablespoon, in all	½ teaspoon ground black pepper
1 tablespoon sliced chives	1 tablespoon fine dry bread crumbs
1 tablespoon finely chopped parsley	⅛ teaspoon paprika

Preheat oven to 350 degrees. In a small bowl, combine cheese, mushrooms, ¼ cup yogurt, chives and parsley. Place each chicken breast between two pieces of clear plastic wrap. Working from the center to the edges, pound lightly with a meat mallet. Remove plastic wrap. Repeat with remaining chicken. Sprinkle lightly with salt and black pepper. Spread equal amounts of the cheese mixture on each chicken breast. Fold in the sides and roll up. Arrange rolls, seam side down, in a 10x6x2-inch baking dish. Brush chicken with the remaining 1 tablespoon yogurt and sprinkle with bread crumbs and paprika. Bake 25 minutes or until chicken is tender.

Chef Chris Oncale

Chicken Sauce Piquant

 Makes 4 to 6 servings

1 (2½ to 3 pound) chicken, cut in serving-sized pieces
1½ tablespoons poultry seasoning
1 tablespoon vegetable oil
1½ cups chopped onion
½ cup chopped green bell pepper

4 cloves garlic, chopped
1 (10 ounce) can tomatoes with green chilies
1 (8 ounce) can tomato sauce
½ cup water
Hot cooked rice

Sprinkle chicken evenly with seasoning. In a large pot over high heat, heat oil. Add chicken and cook about 3 minutes or until browned on all sides. Remove chicken from pot and set aside. Combine onion, bell pepper and garlic in pot. Cook and stir 10 minutes or until vegetables are tender. Return chicken to pot and add tomatoes, tomato sauce and water. Reduce heat to low and cook 40 minutes or until chicken is tender. Serve over rice.

Chef Sonny Aymond

Honey Picante Chicken Wings

Makes 4 servings

16	chicken wings	2	cloves minced garlic
½	cup honey	¼	teaspoon Worcestershire
½	cup picante sauce		sauce

Preheat oven to 350 degrees. Place chicken wings in baking dish. In a small sauce pan, combine picante sauce, garlic and Worcestershire sauce. Cook over medium heat about 5 to 7 minutes. Pour over chicken wings. Bake 30 minutes or until golden brown, coating wings with mixture often.

Chef Donald Hebert

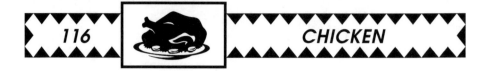
Marinated Lemon Barbecued Chicken

 Makes 4 servings

8	skinless and boneless large chicken breast halves	1	teaspoon paprika
1	cup vegetable oil	2	teaspoons onion powder
½	cup fresh lemon juice	½	teaspoon thyme
1	tablespoon salt	½	teaspoon garlic powder

Place chicken breast in baking dish. Combine oil, lemon juice, salt, paprika, onion powder, thyme and garlic powder. Mix well and pour over chicken breast. Cover dish with plastic wrap and refrigerate 6 to 8 hours or overnight. Place chicken on hot grill. Cook 5 to 7 minutes, brushing often with the marinade, until chicken is golden brown.

Chef Donald Hebert

Chicken in Tomato Basil

 Makes 4 servings

3   cups uncooked pasta
½   cup white wine
½   (6 ounce) can tomato paste
1   (10 ounce) can tomatoes
    with green chilies
1   (6 ounce) can tomato juice
½   cup chicken stock or ½ cup
    water with 1 tablespoon
    chicken bouillon granules
1   tablespoon dried basil leaves,
    crushed, or 2 tablespoons
    fresh chopped basil

1   tablespoon butter or
    margarine
1   pound boneless chicken
    breast, cut in 1 inch strips
1   cup thinly sliced fresh
    mushrooms
¼   cup finely chopped green
    onion
¼   teaspoon salt (optional)

Cook pasta according to package directions and set aside. In a medium bowl, combine wine and tomato paste, tomatoes, tomato juice, bouillon and basil, stirring well to mix. In a large skillet over high heat, melt butter. Add chicken and cook and stir 3 minutes. Add mushrooms and green onion. Cook and stir 2 minutes. Add tomato wine mixture and cooked pasta. Cook and stir 10 minutes or until sauce is desired consistency.

Chef Enola Prudhomme

Christen's Chicken and Sausage Pot Pie

 Makes 6 servings

Filling:

1½ teaspoons salt	½ cup finely chopped green bell pepper
½ teaspoon ground red pepper	½ cup finely chopped red bell pepper
½ teaspoon ground white pepper	½ cup thinly sliced celery
1 pound skinless and boneless chicken breast halves	½ cup milk
6 ounces smoked pork sausage	1 cup heavy whipping cream
¼ cup butter or margarine	½ cup finely chopped green onion
1 cup finely chopped onion	2 tablespoons chopped parsley

Pastry:

4 cups all-purpose flour	1 cup butter or margarine, softened
1 tablespoon salt	2 cups (8 ounces) shredded sharp Cheddar cheese
½ teaspoon ground white pepper	2 cups sour cream
½ teaspoon ground red pepper	

Filling:

In a small bowl, combine salt, red and white pepper, mixing well. Sprinkle mixture over both sides of the chicken. Place over hot grill and cook 5 minutes on each side. Dice chicken and set aside. Remove casing from sausage, dice and set aside. In a medium skillet over high heat, melt butter. Add onion, bell pepper and celery. Cook and stir 10 minutes. Stir in the milk and cream. Reduce heat to medium. Add chicken and sausage. Cook 10 minutes, stirring occasionally. Add green onion and parsley. Cook and stir an additional 10 minutes or until sauce thickens.

Pastry:

In a large bowl, combine flour, salt, white pepper and red pepper, mixing well. Stir in the butter or margarine, cheese and sour cream, mixing well. Mix until dough forms a ball; dough should be smooth and have a

(Chicken and Sausage Pot Pie continued on next page)

(Chicken and Sausage Pot Pie continued)

lot of elasticity. (I use my hands to mix because it works well for me.) Place dough on floured surface and roll out with a rolling pin to fit into a 12x9x2-inch baking dish. Press dough into bottom and sides of the baking dish, trimming edges. Roll out the remaining dough, then cut into 9x12-inch strips and reserve for top crust.

Assemble:
Preheat oven to 375 degrees. Fill baking dish with chicken and sausage mixture. Arrange dough strips on top of mixture to form top crust. Bake 30 minutes, increase heat to 400 degrees and bake an additional 35 minutes.

Chef Enola Prudhomme

Chicken in Mushroom Wine Sauce

Makes 4 servings

¼ cup butter or margarine	1 teaspoon salt
1½ cups chopped onion	2 teaspoons ground black
¾ cup chopped green bell	pepper
pepper	¾ cup white wine
¾ cup chopped red bell	4 cups sliced mushrooms
pepper	2 (10¾ ounce) cans cream of
2 tablespoons diced celery	mushroom soup, undiluted
1 tablespoon minced garlic	8 skinless and boneless
1 tablespoon Worcestershire	chicken breast halves
sauce	½ cup water

In a 5-quart pot over high heat, melt butter. Add onion, bell pepper, celery, garlic, Worcestershire, salt and black pepper. Cook 5 minutes, stirring often. Add wine, mushrooms and soup. Cook and stir 3 minutes. Place chicken in pot and, using a spoon, push pieces to bottom. Reduce heat to medium-high. Add water and cook 7 to 10 minutes longer or until chicken is done, stirring often.

Chef Chris Oncale

Creamy Smothered Chicken

Makes 4 servings

If you would like to reduce the fat and calories in this dish, substitute boneless and skinless chicken breast, vegetable cooking spray instead of oil and fat-free cream cheese. You'll never taste what's missing!

1	tablespoon Enola's Special Seasoning	1	cup chopped red bell pepper
1	(3 to 4 pound) chicken, cut in serving-sized pieces	2	tablespoons all-purpose flour
2	tablespoons vegetable oil	2	(10½ ounce) cans double strength beef broth
1	cup sliced fresh mushrooms	1	tablespoon paprika
1	cup chopped onion	1	(3 ounce) package cream cheese
½	cup chopped green bell pepper		Hot cooked rice or pasta

Sprinkle seasoning evenly over all sides of chicken and set aside. In a 5-quart pot over high heat, heat oil until very hot. Add chicken and cook and stir 5 minutes or until chicken is browned on all sides. Add mushrooms, onion and bell pepper. Cook and stir 5 minutes. Sprinkle flour over chicken, 1 tablespoon at a time, stirring constantly. Reduce heat to medium. Add broth and paprika. Cover and cook 20 minutes, stirring occasionally. Add cream cheese and cook an additional 5 minutes or until cream cheese is dissolved and gravy is nice and smooth. Serve over rice or pasta.

Chef Enola Prudhomme

Country Fried Chicken

 Makes 4 to 6 servings

2 eggs, beaten	4 cups all-purpose flour
1 (12-ounce) can evaporated milk	1 tablespoon plus 1 teaspoon Enola's Special Seasoning
1 (2½ pound) fryer	Vegetable oil
2 tablespoons prepared mustard	

In a small bowl, combine eggs and milk. Mix well and set aside.

Cut chicken in serving sized pieces. Coat well with mustard, then add Enola's seasoning. Sprinkle evenly over meat. Dredge chicken in flour, then in egg mixture and back in flour. Cook in hot oil in skillet until golden brown on all sides, remove and drain on paper towel.

Chef Enola Prudhomme

MEATS

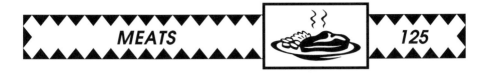

Smothered Diced Pork Roast

 Makes 4 to 6 servings

1 pound boneless pork roast, diced	½ cup chopped green bell pepper
1½ teaspoons salt	½ cup chopped red bell pepper
½ teaspoon ground red pepper	
¼ teaspoon garlic	2 cups water
2 tablespoons vegetable oil	Hot cooked rice
2 cups chopped onion	

Season pork with salt, red pepper and garlic. In a 4-quart pot over high heat, heat oil until very hot. Add pork and cook and stir 7 minutes or until pork is browned on all sides. Add the onion and bell pepper. Cook and stir 10 minutes or until vegetables are transparent. Add water. Reduce heat to medium. Cover and cook 40 minutes or until pork is tender, stirring occasionally. Serve over rice.

Chef Sonny Aymond

Oven Baked Pork Chops with Sonny's Barbecue Sauce

 Makes 4 servings

1 tablespoon butter or margarine, melted	4 center-cut pork chops, about ¾-inch thick
1 tablespoon pork and veal seasoning	2 cups Sonny's Barbecue Sauce (Page 188)

Preheat oven to 350 degrees. Spread butter or margarine in a shallow baking dish. Sprinkle seasoning over both sides of pork chops and place in baking dish. Add barbecue sauce. Cover and bake 20 minutes; uncover and bake an additional 10 minutes.

Chef Sonny Aymond

Three Pepper Pork Chop

 Makes 4 to 6 servings

1 tablespoon granulated garlic	3 tablespoons vegetable oil
1 tablespoon ground mustard	2 ounces julienne-cut green bell pepper
1 tablespoon paprika	2 ounces julienne-cut red bell pepper
1 teaspoon celery salt	
½ teaspoon ground ginger	2 ounces julienne-cut yellow bell pepper
1 teaspoon ground oregano	
1 teaspoon basil leaves, crushed	4 ounces sliced onion
1 teaspoon salt	2 teaspoons reserved seasoning mix
6 center-cut pork chops	1½ cups water
1 cup plus 2 teaspoons all-purpose flour, in all	Hot cooked rice or pasta

In a small bowl, combine garlic, mustard, paprika, salt, ginger, oregano, basil and salt, mixing well. Sprinkle each pork chop evenly on both sides with 3 tablespoons plus 2 teaspoons of the seasoning mix. Place 1 cup flour in bowl and dredge pork chops in flour. In a large skillet over high heat, heat oil until very hot. Add pork chops and cook 5 minutes on each side or until browned on both sides. Add the remaining 2 teaspoons flour and 2 teaspoons seasoning mix, stirring well to mix. Add bell pepper and onion. Cook and stir 15 minutes. Add water. Cook an additional 10 minutes or until pork chops are tender and sauce is thickened. Serve over cooked rice or cooked pasta.

Chef Enola Prudhomme

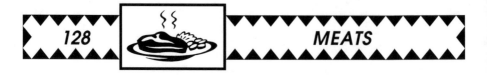

Pork Chops with Gingersnap Gravy

 *Makes 6 servings*

1 teaspoon paprika	1 pound lean pork chops, cut 1-inch thick
1 teaspoon salt	
½ teaspoon ground white pepper	1 cup chopped onion
½ teaspoon ground black pepper	½ cup chopped green bell pepper
⅛ teaspoon dry mustard	½ cup chopped red bell pepper
⅛ teaspoon ground coriander	1½ cups beef stock or water, in all
⅛ teaspoon ground nutmeg	
2 tablespoons vegetable oil	5 gingersnap cookies
	3 cups hot cooked rice

Combine paprika, salt, white pepper, black pepper, mustard, coriander and nutmeg in a small bowl, mixing well. Sprinkle over both sides of pork chops. Place oil in a large skillet over medium heat. Add pork chops and cook 2 minutes on each side, turning often. Add the onion, bell pepper and 1 cup stock or water. Cook and stir 15 minutes. Add the remaining ½ cup stock and gingersnaps. Cook and stir until gingersnaps are dissolved. Serve over rice.

Chef Enola Prudhomme

Marinated Pork Grillades

 Makes 4 to 6 servings

2½ pounds lean pork meat, cut in 2x2-inch cubes
2 tablespoons Enola Special Seasoning
2 tablespoons balsamic vinegar
2 tablespoons vegetable oil
2 cups finely chopped onion
1 cup finely chopped green bell pepper
2½ cups water, in all

In a medium bowl, combine meat, seasoning and vinegar. Cover and place in refrigerate 2 to 3 hours. In a 5-quart pot over high heat, combine oil and meat. Brown on all sides, about 10 minutes. Add onions and bell pepper. Cook 10 minutes, stirring often, or until vegetables and meat are browned. Add 2 cups water. Cover and cook 30 minutes or until meat is tender. Add the remaining ½ cup water. Cook and stir an additional 5 minutes to make a gravy.

Chef Enola Prudhomme

Smothered Pork Chop with Tomato Chilies

Makes 4 servings

1	tablespoon plus 1 teaspoon granulated garlic, in all
1	teaspoon salt
¼	teaspoon ground white pepper
¼	teaspoon ground red pepper
¼	teaspoon ground black pepper
½	teaspoon dried basil leaves, crushed
½	teaspoon dried oregano leaves, crushed
4	center-cut pork chops, cut 1-inch thick
2	tablespoons vegetable oil
1	cup finely chopped onion
½	cup finely chopped green bell pepper
2½	cups finely chopped red bell pepper
1	tablespoon all-purpose flour
½	teaspoon browning and seasoning sauce
1	(10 ounce) can diced tomatoes with green chilies
½	cup beef broth or water
	Hot cooked rice or pasta

In a small bowl, combine 1 tablespoon garlic, salt, white pepper, red pepper, black pepper, basil and oregano, mixing well. Sprinkle seasoning over both sides of pork chops. In a medium skillet over high heat, heat oil until very hot. Add pork chops and cook 5 minutes on each side or until browned. Add onion and bell pepper. Cook and stir 10 minutes. Sprinkle flour over meat. Stir in browning sauce, tomatoes with chilies, broth or water and remaining 1 teaspoon garlic. Cook and stir 10 minutes or until meat is tender and gravy is nice and thickened. Serve over rice or pasta.

Chef Enola Prudhomme

Over-Stuffed Pork Chop

Makes 4 servings

 Yum! Yum!

4	center cut pork chops, cut 1-inch thick	2	tablespoons Worcestershire sauce
½	finely chopped onion	2	teaspoons salt, in all
⅓	finely chopped green bell pepper	1	teaspoon ground white pepper
⅓	finely chopped red bell pepper	2	teaspoons paprika
		½	pound fresh ground pork
		½	pound fresh ground beef

Preheat oven to 375 degrees. On a flat surface, using a sharp knife, make a slit lengthwise in each pork chop and set aside. Place the onion, bell pepper and Worcestershire sauce in a food processor and puree. In a small bowl, combine salt, white pepper and paprika. Mix well and divide into two equal portions. In a large bowl, combine half of seasonings, pureed mixture, pork and beef, using hand to mix well. Divide the mixture in 4 equal amounts and over-stuff each pork chop. Place stuffed pork chops in a 12x9x2-inch baking dish. Sprinkle remaining seasoning on both sides of each pork chop. Bake 40 minutes or until browned. Serve with rice dressing and candied yams.

Chef Chris Oncale

Stuffed Pork Chops

 *Makes 6 servings*

½	cup butter or margarine	6	ounces andouille, finely chopped
1	cup finely chopped onion		
½	cup finely chopped green bell pepper	6	ounces tasso, finely chopped
½	cup finely chopped celery	8	ounces ground beef
3	teaspoons Enola's special seasoning, in all	6	pork chops, cut 1-inch thick
		1	egg
		¾	cup dry, plain bread crumbs

Preheat oven to 350 degrees. In a 8-quart sauce pan over medium heat, melt butter or margarine. Add onion, bell pepper and celery. Cook and stir 5 minutes. Add 1 teaspoon Enola's seasoning and stir well. Cook 5 minutes or until onions are transparent. Add andouille and tasso. Cook and stir 5 minutes. Add beef and 1 teaspoon Enola's seasoning. Cook and stir 10 minutes or until beef is browned. Set aside to cool. Cut a pocket lengthwise in each pork chop. Sprinkle remaining 1 teaspoon seasoning over both sides evenly and set aside. When stuffing mixture is completely cooled, add egg and bread crumbs, mixing well. Stuff each pork chop with ½ cup of stuffing. Place in baking dish. Bake 25 to 30 minutes. Serve immediately.

Chef Donald Hebert

Smothered Pork Chops with Fresh Tomatoes

Makes 4 servings

 This dish is great served over hot cooked rice or pasta!

1 tablespoon salt	½ cup finely chopped celery
½ teaspoon ground white pepper	2 cups water, in all
½ teaspoon ground red pepper	1 tablespoon Worcestershire sauce
4 (8 ounce) center cut-pork chops	1 teaspoon browning seasoning sauce
2 tablespoons vegetable oil	1 cup peeled, seeded and chopped fresh tomatoes
2 cups finely chopped onion	
1 cup finely chopped green bell pepper	

In a small bowl, combine salt, white pepper and red pepper, mixing well. Sprinkle over both sides of pork chops and set aside. Place oil in a medium skillet over high heat and heat until very hot. Add pork chops and cook 5 minutes on each side or until golden brown. Add onion, bell pepper and celery. Cook 10 minutes, stirring often to prevent sticking. Stir in 1 cup water, Worcestershire sauce and browning sauce. Cook and stir 10 minutes. Add tomatoes and continue to cook and stir 10 minutes. Stir in remaining 1 cup water and cook 10 minutes longer or until pork is tender.

Chef Enola Prudhomme

Boneless Pork Loin

 *Makes 4 servings*

1 tablespoon salt	3 tablespoons butter or
2 teaspoons granulated garlic	margarine
½ teaspoon ground red pepper	½ cup sliced onion
¼ teaspoon ground black	½ cup sliced red bell pepper
pepper	½ cup sliced green bell pepper
3 tablespoons Worcestershire	1 medium apple, peeled and
sauce	sliced
1 (2 pound) pork loin	½ cup apple juice
	1 teaspoon all-purpose flour

Preheat oven to 375 degrees. In a small bowl, combine salt, garlic, red pepper and black pepper, mixing well. Set aside. Place roast on flat surface and cut slits in surface. Sprinkle with 1 tablespoon plus 1 teaspoon of seasoning, rubbing with fingertips. Reserve remaining seasoning. Sprinkle Worcestershire sauce over entire roast and set aside. In a medium skillet over high heat, heat butter until very hot. Add onion, bell pepper and apples. Cook and stir 5 minutes. Add 1 tablespoon reserved seasoning. Dissolve flour in apple juice and add to mixture. Cook and stir 10 minutes. Remove from heat and let cool to touch. Open slits and fill with apple onion mixture. Spray baking dish with vegetable spray. Bake, uncovered, 30 minutes; cover and cook additional 45 minutes or until roast is tender.

Chef Enola Prudhomme

"Mac Daddy" Venison Roast

Makes 6 servings

 "Mac Daddy refers to " the best of the best", a term Sonny picked up from his kids. It means this is really great! If you can't get venison, beef is a fine substitute.

1	(6 to 8 pound) venison roast	1½	tablespoons salt
1	cup chopped onion	1	tablespoon salt-free lemon
1	cup white wine		pepper seasoning
1	cup water	1	teaspoon ground red pepper
2	tablespoons minced garlic		

Using a sharp knife, cut 6 to 8 slits about 2 inches long and 2 to 3 inches deep over entire roast. In a medium bowl, combine remaining ingredients. Add seasoning mixture to roast by stuffing the pockets on all sides. Place roast in a large covered container and refrigerate overnight to marinate. Remove roast and discard marinade. Preheat oven to 350 degrees. Put roast in a browning bag and place in a 13x9x2-inch baking dish. Bake 2½ to 3 hours or until the meat pulls away from the bone.

Chef Sonny Aymond

Chicken-Fried Venison Strips

 *Makes 6 servings*

2	pounds venison steaks, cut ½-inch thick	2	eggs
½	teaspoon salt	½	cup milk
½	teaspoon ground red pepper	3	cups vegetable oil
		2	cups all-purpose flour

Cut venison steaks in ¼ -inch strips. Sprinkle with salt and red pepper. Refrigerate for 2 hours to marinate. Beat together eggs and milk and set aside. In a large skillet over medium heat, heat the oil. Remove meat from refrigerator. Dip each strip in egg mixture and dredge in flour, coating well. Shake off excess flour and fry in hot oil until golden brown.

Chef Sonny Aymond

Cajun Meat Jambalaya

 Makes 6 to 8 servings

3	tablespoons vegetable oil	1	cup chopped green onion
½	pound mixed sausage, cut in bite-sized pieces	½	cup chopped celery
½	pound pork tasso, thinly sliced	1	teaspoon minced garlic
1	pound chicken breast, cubed	1	tablespoon salt
6	ounces smoked ham, cubed	½	teaspoon ground red pepper
1½	cups chopped onion	1	(15 ounce) can tomato sauce
		4	cups chicken stock or broth
		5	cups cooked rice

In a 8-quart pot over high heat, heat oil until very hot. Add sausage, tasso, chicken and ham. Cook and stir 10 minutes. Add onion, green onion, celery, garlic, salt and red pepper, stirring to prevent burning. Add tomato sauce and stock or broth. Cook, stirring occasionally, 15 minutes. Reduce heat to simmer and cook an additional 15 minutes or until meat is tender. Mixture should have lots of liquid. Add cooked rice, stirring to incorporate thoroughly. Serve hot.

Chef Enola Prudhomme

Rabbit Stew

Makes 4 to 6 servings

 A black cast iron pot works well; it is my favorite.

2 teaspoons salt	½ cup chopped green bell pepper
1½ teaspoons ground red pepper	¼ cup chopped celery
2 teaspoons granulated garlic	3 cups water
1 (3 pound) rabbit, cut in serving pieces	½ cup chopped green onion
¾ cup all-purpose flour, in all	¼ cup chopped parsley
½ cup vegetable oil	Hot cooked rice
1 cup chopped onion	

In a small bowl, combine salt, red pepper and garlic, mixing well. Sprinkle over rabbit. Dredge pieces in ½ cup flour. In a heavy 8-quart pot, heat oil until very hot. Add rabbit and brown on all sides, remove rabbit and set aside. In the same pot, stir in remaining ¼ cup flour and cook, stirring constantly, for 5 minutes or until roux is the color of peanut butter. Reduce heat to medium. Stir in onion, bell pepper and celery. Cook and stir 10 minutes or until vegetables are tender. Return browned rabbit to pot. Add water, bring to a boil, reduce heat and simmer 10 minutes. Add green onion and parsley and cook additional 8 minutes. Serve over rice.

Chef Sonny Aymond

Sonny's Smothered Squirrel

 *Makes 4 servings*

1	teaspoon salt	½	cup finely chopped green bell pepper
½	teaspoon ground red pepper	¼	cup finely chopped celery
2	squirrels, cut in serving pieces	1	tablespoon minced garlic
¼	cup vegetable oil	5	cups water
1	cup finely chopped onion		Hot cooked rice

Sprinkle salt and red pepper evenly over meat. In a large cast-iron pot over high heat, heat oil until very hot. Add the meat and brown on all sides. Add the onion, bell pepper, celery and garlic. Cook and stir 5 minutes or until onions are transparent. Add the water. Cover, bring to a boil and cook 10 minutes. Reduce heat to low and continue cooking, covered, 1 hour or until meat is tender. Serve over rice.

Chef Sonny Aymond

Beef Chili

 Makes 8 servings

1	tablespoon vegetable oil	2	(16 ounce) cans diced tomatoes
2	pounds ground beef	1	(6 ounce) can tomato paste
1½	cups chopped onion	2	cloves garlic, minced
1	cup chopped green bell pepper	2	tablespoons chili powder
2	(15 ounce) cans red kidney beans	1	teaspoon salt
		¼	teaspoon ground red pepper
		1	cup water

In a 8-quart pot over high heat, combine oil, ground beef, onion and bell pepper. Cook and stir 15 minutes or until ground beef is browned and vegetables are tender. Add beans, tomatoes, tomato paste, garlic, chili powder, salt, red pepper and water. Reduce heat to medium, cover and cook 15 minutes, stirring occasionally. Reduce heat to simmer, cover and continue cooking 20 minutes. Serve hot with crackers or bread sticks.

Chef Sonny Aymond

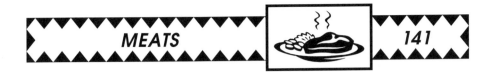

Quick and Easy After-Practice Casserole

Makes 6 servings

 I used corn in this recipe but you can substitute sweet peas or green beans.

1	(8 ounce) package egg noodles
1	tablespoon vegetable oil
1½	pounds ground beef
½	cup finely chopped onion
⅓	cup finely chopped green bell pepper
½	teaspoon salt
¼	teaspoon ground red pepper
1	(15 ounce) can whole kernel corn
1	(10¾ ounce) can cream of chicken soup, undiluted
1	(10¾ ounce) can cream of mushroom soup, undiluted
1	cup sour cream
1	cup Italian style bread crumbs
4	slices cheese

Preheat oven to 350 degrees. Cook egg noodles according to package directions, drain, and set aside. In an 8-quart pot over high heat, combine oil and ground beef. Cook and stir 10 minutes. Add onion and bell pepper. Cook 8 minutes or until onions are transparent. Add salt, red pepper, corn, soups and sour cream, stirring to mix well. Reduce heat to low and cook 5 minutes, stirring occasionally. Add cooked egg noodles, stirring to mix well. Pour mixture into 12x9x2-inch baking dish. Sprinkle bread crumbs evenly over top and finish with single layer of cheese. Bake 8 to 10 minutes or until cheese is melted.

Chef Sonny Aymond

Smothered Sirloin Tip Steak

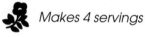

Makes 4 servings

1½ tablespoons meat seasoning
1 teaspoon salt
1 pound beef sirloin tip steak, trimmed
2 tablespoons vegetable oil
2 cups coarsely chopped onion

½ cup finely chopped green bell pepper
½ cup finely chopped red bell pepper
1½ cups beef stock or water

In a small bowl, combine seasoning and salt. Sprinkle over both sides of the meat and set aside. In a large Dutch oven over high heat, heat oil until very hot. Add meat and cook 5 minutes on both sides or until browned. Add onion and bell pepper. Cook and stir 10 minutes. Add stock or water and cook, uncovered, 30 minutes or until meat is tender, stirring often.

Chef Sonny Aymond

All-in-One
Beef and Rice Casserole

Makes 10 servings

 If this recipe is too large, just freeze half. The next time you have unexpected guests or you had to work real late, just defrost, heat and enjoy.

1	tablespoon vegetable oil	1	(16 ounce) can tomato sauce
1	pound ground beef	1	packet dry onion soup
1	cup finely chopped onion	2½	teaspoons meat seasoning
¼	cup finely chopped green bell pepper	1	(10¾ ounce) can cream of mushroom soup, undiluted
½	cup finely chopped red bell pepper	1	cup uncooked rice
		12	slices of cheese, in all

Preheat oven to 350 degrees. In an 8-quart pot over high heat, combine oil and meat. Sauté 5 minutes or until meat is browned. Add onion and bell pepper. Sauté 8 minutes. Add tomato sauce, onion soup, meat seasoning and mushroom soup, stirring to mix well. Add rice and 4 slices of cheese, mixing well. Spoon mixture into 10x10x2-inch baking pan. Bake, covered, for 1 hour; remove from oven, top with remaining cheese and bake 3 minutes or until cheese is melted.

Chef Sonny Aymond

Pan-Sautéed Steak Annette

 Makes 6 servings

1 tablespoon plus 1 teaspoon
Enola's Special Seasoning
2 pounds beef tenderloin, cut
in ½-inch filets
3 tablespoons unsalted butter
1 cup (about 3 ounces)
shiitake mushrooms

1 cup thinly sliced onion
1 cup demi glace or double
strength beef broth
½ cup Marsala wine (optional)
1 cup heavy whipping cream

Sprinkle seasoning on both sides of each filet. In a heavy skillet over high heat, melt butter. Place steaks in skillet, sear on both sides, remove from skillet and keep warm. In the same skillet, combine mushrooms, onion and broth. Sauté 5 minutes or until onions are transparent. Add wine and cook 3 minutes. Add cream. Cook and stir an additional 4 to 5 minutes or until sauce is thickened. If you like your steaks well done or medium well, place meat back in skillet and cook until desired doneness. Spoon sauce on a plate and place steak over sauce.

Chef Enola Prudhomme

Beef Stroganoff the Chef's Way

 *Makes 4 servings*

1	pound boneless beef chuck steak	2	teaspoons ground black pepper
1¼	cups sour cream	2	cups sliced fresh mushrooms
3	tablespoons all-purpose flour	½	cup finely chopped onion
1½	teaspoons beef bouillon granules	2	tablespoons butter or margarine
2	teaspoons Worcestershire sauce	½	cup beef stock or broth
		2½	cups hot cooked egg noodles

Slice meat across the grain into bite-sized strips. In a small bowl, stir together sour cream and flour. Stir in bouillon granules, Worcestershire sauce and black pepper. Set aside. In a large skillet over medium heat, sauté mushrooms and onion in butter until tender. Remove from skillet. Add beef to skillet and cook 4 minutes or until meat is browned; remove from skillet. Add stock or broth to skillet and bring to a boil. Stir in sour cream mixture. Return meat, mushrooms and onion to skillet. Cook and stir 10 minutes or until thickened. Serve over noodles.

Chef Chris Oncale

Rolled Round Steak

Makes 4 servings

1	(4 pound) round steak	1	pound ground beef
3	tablespoons meat seasoning, in all	½	cup Worcestershire sauce
1	tablespoon pork and veal seasoning	¾	cup mildly hot and sweet sauce
2	cups thinly sliced green bell pepper	1	link smoked mixed sausage
		2½	cups finely chopped onion
2	cups thinly sliced red bell pepper	2	tablespoons vegetable oil
		2	cups water
			Hot cooked rice

Place round steak on clean surface, sprinkle 2 tablespoons meat seasoning evenly over both sides and set aside. In a medium bowl, combine remaining 1 tablespoon seasoning, bell pepper, ground beef, Worcestershire sauce and hot and sweet sauce, stirring well to mix. Spread meat mixture evenly over steak. Place sausage in middle of steak and roll up, jelly roll style. Place steak, seam side down, and tie with cooking string. In a 5-quart pot over high heat, heat oil until hot. Add rolled steak and onion. Cook 10 minutes, turning steak often and making sure steak is browned on all sides. Add water. Cover, reduce heat to medium and cook 30 minutes. Serve over rice.

Chef Sonny Aymond

Cajun Enchiladas

 Makes 4 servings

2	tablespoons vegetable oil	½	(8 ounce) box pasteurized processed cheese, cubed
1	pound ground beef		
¼	cup very finely chopped onion	1	teaspoon cornstarch
		½	cup beef stock or water
1	tablespoon Worcestershire sauce	4	hot dried chili peppers, crushed
1½	tablespoon salt	1	teaspoon dried oregano leaves, crushed
1½	cups heavy whipping cream, in all	½	teaspoon ground cumin
1	(4 ounce) can chopped mild chili peppers, undrained	8	(6 inch) flour tortillas
		½	cup (2 ounces) shredded Cheddar cheese

In a large skillet over high heat, heat oil until very hot. Add beef and cook 10 minutes stirring often. Add onion, Worcestershire and salt. Cook and stir 5 minutes. Transfer mixture to a bowl and set aside. In same skillet over high heat, combine 1 cup cream, canned chili peppers and cheese. Cook, stirring constantly, until cheese is melted. Dissolve cornstarch in stock or water and stir into cheese mixture. Combine dried chili pepper, oregano, meat mixture, cumin and the remaining ½ cup cream. Cook and stir 5 minutes or until sauce thickens. Remove from heat and set aside. Preheat oven to 350 degrees. In a small iron skillet over medium heat, brown tortillas for 30 seconds on each side. Spoon ¼ cup filling across center of each tortilla. Fold in thirds to enclose the filling and place seam side down in a 9x9x2-inch ungreased baking dish. Spoon remaining sauce over tortilla and top with cheddar cheese. Bake 15 minutes or until cheese is melted.

Chef Enola Prudhomme

Brandied Tenderloin Medallion

 Makes 4 to 6 servings

1	(16 ounce) package angel hair pasta	¼	cup butter or margarine
1½	pounds beef tenderloins, cut in 2-ounce medallions	1	cup sliced fresh mushrooms
		¾	cup chopped green onion
1	tablespoon cracked black pepper	½	cup beef stock or beef broth
		¼	teaspoon salt
⅔	cup brandy, in all	⅛	teaspoon cayenne pepper
		¼	cup heavy whipping cream

Cook angel hair pasta as directed on package, rinse and set aside. Sprinkle medallions with cracked black pepper. Pound lightly and place in bowl. Add 2 tablespoons brandy. Let marinate in refrigerator 30 minutes. In a large skillet over medium heat, melt butter for about 1 minute. Remove from heat. Place medallions in skillet and return to heat. (Caution: Brandy may flame. If this happens, cover 10 to 15 seconds to extinguish.) Cook until medium rare. Remove medallions and place on platter in warm oven. In the same skillet over high heat, combine mushrooms, green onion, stock or broth, salt and cayenne pepper. Cook over high heat for 5 minutes. Add remaining brandy and whipping cream. Cook and stir 3 minutes or until sauce thickens. Place medallions on angel hair pasta and pour brandy cream sauce on top.

Chef Donald Hebert

Sonny's Oven Baked Brisket

 Makes 12 to 14 servings

2	tablespoons salt	1	tablespoon liquid smoke
2	tablespoons onion powder	⅓	cup bottled steak sauce
1	tablespoon ground black pepper	½	cup red wine vinegar
1½	teaspoons ground white pepper	2	cups finely chopped onion
½	teaspoons ground red pepper	½	cup finely chopped green bell pepper
1	(7 pound) beef brisket	½	cup finely chopped red bell pepper

In a small bowl, combine salt, onion powder, black pepper, white pepper and red pepper, mixing well. Using a sharp knife, make several 1½-inch slits in the brisket. Sprinkle some of the seasoning inside each slit, then rub the remaining seasoning over the outside surface of the meat and place in a large bowl. In a small bowl, combine liquid smoke, steak sauce and vinegar. Drizzle mixture over the meat; cover and refrigerate overnight. Place meat and marinade in a large baking dish with the onion and bell pepper. Preheat oven to 350 degrees. Cover and bake 3½ hours or until tender, basting occasionally. Transfer the meat to a platter and cut into slices.

Chef Sonny Aymond

Smothered Liver

Makes 4 servings

 You can serve this dish with rice or grits.

1 tablespoon salt	1 medium-sized onion, cut julienne
1½ teaspoons ground white pepper	1 medium-sized green bell pepper, cut julienne
¼ teaspoon granulated garlic	1 medium-sized red bell pepper, cut julienne
1 cup all-purpose flour	
1 pound fresh veal liver	
½ cup vegetable oil	1 cup water

In a small bowl, combine salt, white pepper and garlic, mixing well. Sprinkle over both sides of liver. Put flour into a bowl and dredge liver in flour, coating well. In a medium skillet over high heat, heat oil until very hot. Add liver and cook 10 minutes or until browned on both sides, turning often. Add onions and bell peppers. Cook 5 minutes or until vegetables are tender, scraping bottom of skillet to remove all the goodness. Add water, cover and cook for 15 minutes.

Chef Chris Oncale

Meat-Stuffed Bell Pepper A La Leigh

 *Makes 4 servings*

8 cups water	1 teaspoon ground white pepper
4 large red or green bell peppers	¼ teaspoon very finely chopped jalapeño pepper
2 tablespoon salt, in all	1 (10¾ ounce) can of cream chicken soup, undiluted
1 teaspoon butter or margarine	
½ pound fresh ground beef	1¼ cup fine dry bread crumbs
¼ cup finely chopped celery	10 slices bacon, cut crosswise in ½-inch pieces
½ cup finely chopped red onion	
½ cup finely chopped green bell pepper	¾ cup (3 ounces) shredded Cheddar cheese

Preheat oven to 350 degrees. In a 3-quart pot over high heat, bring water to a boil. Trim tops from bell peppers, reserve tops and place remainder of bell peppers in boiling water with 1 tablespoon salt. Boil 10 minutes. Remove bell peppers from water, drain and place in ice water to cool, about 2 to 3 minutes. Remove from water and place in refrigerator until ready to stuff. In a medium pot over high heat, melt butter. Add ground meat and cook and stir 5 minutes or until browned. Drain any excess grease from meat. Add the celery, onion, bell pepper, remaining 1 tablespoon salt, white pepper and jalapeño. Cook and stir 7 minutes. In same pot, combine chicken soup, bread crumbs, bacon and cheese. Cook and stir 3 minutes. Remove from heat and let cool for 20 minutes. Stuff each bell pepper with equal portion of mixture. Place bell peppers in 12x9x2-inch baking dish. Bake 20 minutes.

Chef Chris Oncale

Veal a la Eli

Makes 4 servings

 This recipe won a silver medal in the Culinary Classics.

⅛ teaspoon salt	1 cup thinly sliced fresh
⅛ teaspoon ground white	mushrooms
pepper	½ cup thinly sliced green
⅛ teaspoon ground red pepper	onions
1 pound fresh veal filets	1½ cups heavy whipping cream
3 tablespoons butter or	1 cup lump crabmeat, picked
margarine	over
⅓ cup finely chopped tasso	½ teaspoon paprika

In a small bowl, mix salt, white pepper and red pepper. Sprinkle over both sides of veal. Spray with vegetable cooking spray. Place on hot grill, cook 2 minutes, turn and cook for 4 minutes. Remove from grill, place on plate and keep warm. In a medium skillet over high heat, combine butter, tasso, mushrooms and green onion. Cook 10 minutes, shaking skillet constantly. Add cream and cook and stir an additional 10 minutes or until cream starts to thicken. Gently stir in crabmeat and paprika. Cook 2 to 3 minutes; do not overcook. Place each filet on a plate and spoon equal portions of the cream sauce over each filet.

Chef Enola Prudhomme

Linda's Sausage Sauce Piquant

Makes 4 servings

 Linda is a friend who works with my wife Radonna. She loves when Radonna shares her lunch with her, especially when it's Sausage Sauce Piquant!

¼	cup vegetable oil	1	teaspoon ground red pepper
1	pound smoked pork sausage, cut into bite-sized pieces	½	teaspoon sugar
		1	(6 ounce) can of tomato paste
2	cups coarsely chopped onion	1½	cups water
1	cup coarsely chopped green bell pepper	2	tablespoons chopped parsley
½	cup finely chopped celery	1	cup chopped green onion
1	teaspoon salt		Hot cooked rice

In a 5-quart pot over high heat, combine oil and sausage. Cook and stir 5 minutes or until sausage starts to brown. Add the onion, bell pepper, celery, salt, red pepper and sugar. Cook and stir for 10 minutes. Add tomato paste and cook and stir 5 minutes. Add water and cook 35 minutes; stirring often. Reduce heat to simmer. Add parsley and green onion. Cook and stir an additional 5 minutes. Remove from heat and let stand a few minutes before serving. Serve over rice.

Chef Sonny Aymond

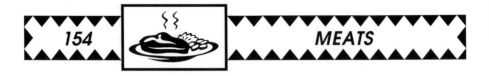

Sausage and Vegetable Kabobs

 Makes 4 servings

1	(12 ounce) package smoked sausage, cut into bite-sized pieces	2	large onion, quartered
		2	large green bell peppers, quartered
12	cherry tomatoes		Barbecue sauce (optional)

Thread sausage, tomato, onion and bell pepper on each skewer. Place on grill and cook for 7 minutes on each side or until vegetables are tender. If desired, baste with barbecue sauce during cooking, turning frequently.

Chef Chris Oncale

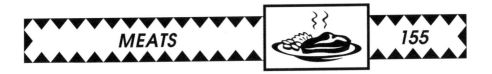

Chris's Special Meat Loaf

 *Makes 1 loaf*

1 egg, beaten	3 tablespoons mildly hot and sweet sauce
1 cup Italian bread crumbs	
⅓ cup grated onion	¼ teaspoon salt
⅓ cup finely chopped green bell pepper	¼ teaspoon ground white pepper
½ cup evaporated milk	¼ teaspoon granulated garlic
	1½ pounds ground beef

Preheat oven to 375 degrees. In a large bowl, combine egg, bread crumbs, onion, bell pepper, milk, hot and sweet sauce, salt, white pepper and garlic, mixing well. Add beef and mix with hands until mixed well. Shape the ground meat into a 9x4x3-inch loaf pan that has been sprayed with vegetable cooking spray. Bake for 1 hour or until meat is browned. Baste loaf with additional mildly hot and sweet sauce after loaf is done, if desired.

Chef Chris Oncale

🌺 Notes

VEGETABLES

Sonny's Super Easy Beans

Makes 10 servings

 This is a great dish to bring to church gatherings or a family reunion. My mother-in-law makes this dish on Sundays when the family gets together and there's always enough left over for us to bring home for supper!

5 **(15½ ounce) cans cut green beans**	¼ **teaspoon Vegetable Seasoning**
½ **cup butter or margarine**	1 **(10¾ ounce) can cream of mushroom soup, undiluted**
1½ **cups finely chopped onion**	
1 **(6 ounce) roll pasteurized processed garlic cheese**	1 **(2 ounce) can French fried onions (optional)**

Preheat range oven to 350 degrees. Place the beans in microwave-safe dish. Place in the microwave oven and cook at high setting 15 minutes. Remove and let stand 3 minutes. Drain liquid from beans and discard; set beans aside. In another microwave-safe dish, combine the butter and onion. Microwave, stirring occasionally, 5 minutes or until onions are tender. Add the cheese, seasoning, mushroom soup and beans, mixing well. Sprinkle the fried onions on top of mixture and bake in range oven 15 minutes.

Chef Sonny Aymond

Cole Slaw—The Oncale Way

Makes 6 servings

 This goes great with fried foods.

½ **medium head green cabbage, shredded**
2 **large carrots, peeled and shredded**

½ **teaspoon salt**
1 **teaspoon finely chopped jalapeño pepper**
1 **cup bottled ranch dressing**

In a medium bowl, combine all ingredients and mix well.

Chef Chris Oncale

Sweet Potato Crunch

Makes 6 servings

4 cups cooked sweet potatoes	¼ teaspoon ground nutmeg
2½ cups sugar	2 cups firmly packed dark brown sugar
1 teaspoon salt	
1 tablespoon vanilla extract	¾ cup all-purpose flour
4 eggs, beaten	2 cups pecans
½ cup butter or margarine, melted and cooled	⅔ cup butter or margarine, melted and cooled
1 cup heavy whipping cream	2 dozen pecan halves for garnish
⅛ teaspoon ground cinnamon	

Preheat oven to 350 degrees. In a medium bowl, mash potatoes with a fork. Add sugar, salt, vanilla, eggs, ½ cup butter or margarine, cream, cinnamon and nutmeg. Mix well. Pour the potato mixture into a 13x9x2-inch baking pan. In a food processor, combine brown sugar, flour, pecans and ⅔ cup butter or margarine. After topping is blended well, spread evenly on top of sweet potato mixture. Place pecan halves on top and bake 10 minutes.

Chef Sonny Aymond

Brady's Candied Yams

 Makes 4 servings

1	(6 ounce) can of orange juice	¼	teaspoon ground nutmeg
1	cup sugar	⅛	teaspoon ground cinnamon
¾	cup firmly packed light brown sugar	⅛	teaspoon salt
2	tablespoons butter or margarine	8	yam patties or 1 (29 ounce) can sweet potatoes

Preheat oven to 350 degrees. In a 5-quart pot over high heat, combine orange juice, sugar, brown sugar, butter or margarine, nutmeg, cinnamon and salt. Cook and stir 5 minutes or until mixture starts to thicken. Place yam patties or sweet potato pieces in 9x9x2-inch baking dish and pour sauce over top. Cover and bake 20 minutes.

Chef Sonny Aymond

Corn Maque Choux

 *Makes 4 servings*

16	ears fresh corn on the cob	1	cup milk
¼	cup vegetable oil	1	cup half-and-half
1	medium-sized onion, finely chopped	3	tablespoons sugar
		1½	teaspoons salt
½	cup finely chopped green bell pepper	¼	teaspoon ground red pepper
½	cup finely chopped red bell pepper	½	cup finely chopped green onion
			Hot cooked rice

Using a sharp knife, cut the top of the kernels from the cob, then cut a second time. Scrape the remaining kernels from the cob with the dull side of the knife and set kernels aside. In a 5-quart Dutch oven over high heat, combine the oil, onion and bell pepper. Cook and stir 10 minutes or until onion is transparent. Reduce heat to medium. Add corn, milk, half-and-half, sugar, salt and red pepper. Cover and cook and stir 10 minutes or until corn is tender. Stir in green onion. Remove from heat and let stand, covered, 5 minutes. Serve over rice for an entree or without rice for a side dish.

Chef Enola Prudhomme

Smothered Turnips

Makes 6 (1 cup) servings

 This is a wonderful dish that freezes well.

1 tablespoon butter or margarine	2 cups water
3½ cups sliced turnips (about 8 small), peeled	1 tablespoon Enola's Special seasoning

In a 5-quart pot over high heat, combine all ingredients. Cover and cook 15 minutes, stirring occasionally.

Chef Enola Prudhomme

Blackeyes with Sausage

 Makes 6 servings

8½ cups water
1½ cups (about 9 ounces) dried black eyed peas
1 tablespoon salt
1 teaspoon ground white pepper
1 tablespoon garlic power

1 tablespoon dried parsley
1 tablespoon paprika
1 cup dried onions
1 pound smoked pork sausage, cut into 1-inch pieces

In a 5-quart pot, combine all ingredients. Bring to boil. Reduce heat to medium and cook 45 minutes or until beans are tender, stirring occasionally. C'est Bon!!

Chef Chris Oncale

Deena's Chunky Potato Salad

Makes 8 (½ cup) servings

 Serve this dish warm or cold.

6 cups water	1 cup mayonnaise
10 medium potatoes, peeled and quartered	1 tablespoon prepared mustard
4 eggs	2 tablespoons sweet relish
1 tablespoon plus 1 teaspoon salt, in all	½ teaspoon ground white or black pepper

Place water, potatoes and eggs in a heavy 5-quart pot over high heat and bring to boil. Add 1 tablespoon salt. Cook 15 to 20 minutes or until potatoes are tender but still firm. Drain. Peel eggs and rinse under cold water. Place in a large bowl and mash well with a fork. Stir in mayonnaise, mustard, relish, white or black pepper and the remaining 1 teaspoon salt. Add potatoes and stir gently until mixed well, leaving potatoes chunky.

Chef Donald Hebert

Boiled Okra

 *Makes 4 servings*

4	cups	1	teaspoon garlic powder
2	teaspoons salt	1	teaspoon onion powder
½	teaspoon ground black pepper	1	pound small, tender whole okra
½	teaspoon ground red pepper		

In a large pot over high heat, combine water, salt, black pepper, red pepper, garlic powder and onion powder. Bring to a boil. Add okra, return to a boil and cook 10 to 12 minutes. Remove okra from water with slotted spoon and serve hot.

Chef Donald Hebert

Rice Dressing

 Makes 4 (1 cup) servings

1 cup water	1½ cups chicken or beef stock
½ pound chicken livers	½ cup chopped green onion
2 tablespoons vegetable oil	3 tablespoons finely chopped
1 cup finely chopped onion	parsley
1 pound lean ground beef	2 cups hot cooked rice
½ teaspoon salt	½ teaspoon browning sauce
¼ teaspoon ground red pepper	

In a 1-quart pot over high heat, bring water to boil. Add chicken livers and boil 5 minutes. Drain, reserving liquid. Allow livers to cool 5 minutes, then chop and set aside. In a 4-quart pot over high heat, heat oil. Add onion. Cook and stir 5 minutes. Add ground beef and cook 10 minutes, stirring often. Add salt, red pepper and liver. Cook 5 minutes. Add stock, green onion and parsley. Cook 5 minutes. Add rice and browning sauce. Stir to mix well.

Chef Sonny Aymond

Fried Green Tomatoes

 *Makes 6 servings*

1 pound green tomatoes	1 cup corn meal
1 tablespoon Vegetable Seasoning, in all	1 cup vegetable oil
½ cup all-purpose flour	1 cup (4 ounces) freshly grated Parmesan cheese

Slice tomatoes ¼-inch thick. Place slices in a one layer on a large cutting board. Sprinkle each slice evenly with Vegetable Seasoning, using about 1½ teaspoons. In a small bowl, combine flour, corn meal and the remaining 1½ teaspoons seasoning. Mix well. Coat sliced tomatoes with flour mixture by pressing with fingers to coat well. Place oil in a medium skillet over high heat and heat until very hot. Place a single layer of tomatoes in skillet (don't over lap). Cook 1 minute or until golden brown, turn over and cook an additional 1 minute. Remove from skillet and drain on paper towel. Sprinkle each slice of tomato with cheese and serve hot.

Chef Enola Prudhomme

Sautéed Vegetables

 Makes 6 servings

4 cups water	6 ounces fresh snow peas
1 pound fresh whole green beans	1 medium-sized red onion, sliced
2 tablespoon vegetable oil	1 (16-ounce) can whole baby corn
1½ cups chopped celery	2 bunches broccoli flowerets
1 small red bell pepper, cut julienne	2 tablespoons Enola's Special Seasoning
1 small green bell pepper, cut julienne	

In a 5-quart pot over high heat, add water and bring to a boil. Add whole beans and cook 10 minutes, just enough to blanch them. Drain and set aside. In a large skillet over high heat, add oil and remaining ingredients. Cook and stir 10 minutes or until vegetables are cooked but still crispy.

Chef Enola Prudhomme

Chris's Fresh Spinach

 Makes 3 (1 cup) servings

1 tablespoon butter or margarine	¼ teaspoon minced garlic
½ cup finely chopped red bell pepper	1 teaspoon salt
	½ teaspoon ground white pepper
½ cup finely chopped red onion	⅛ teaspoon ground red pepper
¼ cup finely chopped celery	¼ cup pork tasso, cut julienne
1 cup finely chopped onion	1 pound fresh spinach, picked over and washed

In a 5-quart pot over high heat, combine butter or margarine, bell pepper, red onion, celery, onion, garlic, salt, white pepper and red pepper. Cook and stir 7 minutes. Add tasso. Cook and stir 2 minutes, then add spinach. Cook and stir 3 additional minutes.

Chef Chris Oncale

Baked Beans

 Makes 4 to 6 servings

8	slices bacon, in all	3	tablespoons light brown sugar
1	large onion, chopped		
1	small green bell pepper, chopped	1½	teaspoons prepared mustard
4	(16-ounce) cans pork and beans	1	teaspoon salt
		⅛	teaspoon ground red pepper
½	cup ketchup	¼	cup Worcestershire sauce

Preheat oven to 350 degrees. In a large skillet over high heat, fry 4 slices bacon until golden browned. Remove from skillet, drain on paper towel and let cool to touch. Crumble and set aside. In same skillet, combine the onion and bell pepper. Cook and stir 7 minutes or until tender. Add beans, crumbled bacon, ketchup, brown sugar, mustard, salt, red pepper, and Worcestershire sauce. Stir well and pour into a 2-quart casserole. Arrange the remaining 4 slices bacon on top and bake 1 hour.

Chef Sonny Aymond

Garlic Roasted Potatoes

 Makes 8 servings

10	medium potatoes, unpeeled and cubed	2	teaspoons salt
1¼	cups butter or margarine	1	teaspoon ground red pepper
1	cup finely chopped onion	1	teaspoon ground black pepper
½	cup finely chopped bell pepper	2	teaspoons garlic powder
½	cup finely chopped celery	2	teaspoons onion powder
2	tablespoons Worcestershire sauce	2	tablespoons chopped parsley
¼	cup fresh chopped garlic	3	tablespoons chopped green onion tops

Preheat oven to 350 degrees. Wash potatoes, drain and set aside. In medium saucepan over high heat, melt margarine. Add onion, bell pepper and celery. Cook 5 minutes over high heat, stirring often. Add Worcestershire sauce, garlic, salt, red pepper, black pepper, garlic powder and onion powder. Cook and stir 5 minutes. Add parsley and onion tops. Place potatoes in 12x7x2-inch baking dish. Pour onion and seasoning mixture over potatoes, stirring to coat well. Bake 25 minutes, stirring every 10 minutes.

Chef Donald Hebert

Broccoli Rice

 Makes 4 servings

3	stalks fresh broccoli	2	tablespoons vegetable oil
1	cup uncooked long grain rice	¼	cup sliced mushrooms
2	cups beef broth	1	cup diced onions
2	cups water	1	cup (4 ounces) processed cheese spread, melted

Peel broccoli stems and slice thinly. Cut off flowerets. Set stem and flowerets aside. Combine rice and broth in 3-quart sauce pan. Cook 15 minutes over medium heat. While rice is cooking, bring water to boil in small saucepan over high heat. Add broccoli and cook 6 minutes. Drain and set aside. Heat oil in 12-inch skillet over medium-high heat. Add mushrooms and onion. Simmer 3 minutes. When rice is cooked, add to vegetables in skillet. Cook over medium heat 5 minutes, stirring often. Pour rice mixture into a serving bowl and top with broccoli. Pour warm cheese over broccoli and serve.

Chef Donald Hebert

Country Quiche

 Makes 8 servings

5 leaves frozen filo dough	1½ cups minced Canadian bacon
Butter-flavored vegetable cooking spray	1 teaspoon ground white pepper
¼ cup plus 2 tablespoons vegetable oil	1½ cups canned evaporated milk
3 tablespoons finely chopped green onions	4 whole eggs
½ cup minced onion	½ cup (2 ounces) shredded Cheddar cheese
2 cups fresh mushrooms, thinly sliced	½ cup (2 ounces) Parmesan cheese

Thaw filo dough by removing from freezer. Place package, unopened, in refrigerator the night before or at least 6 hours before using. Remove from refrigerator and let stand 2 hours at room temperature. Preheat oven to 350 degrees. Remove filo from package. Unroll all filo on flat surface. In a 9-inch pie plate sprayed with butter flavored vegetable spray, place 1 leaf filo dough at a time. Spraying each leaf separately, layer in pie plate to form crust. Trim excess filo around edge of plate with scissors, cover with damp towel and set aside. In a small skillet over high heat, combine oil, green onion, onion, mushrooms, bacon and white pepper. Sauté for 3 minutes or until onions are transparent. Reduce heat to simmer. In a small bowl, combine milk, eggs, Cheddar cheese and Parmesan cheese. Mix well. Add to onion mixture and stir well. Pour into filo crust. Bake 30 minutes.

Chef Enola Prudhomme

Darlee and Moma's Potato Salad

Makes 6 servings

 When I was a kid, mom always made potato salad for Sunday dinners. My oldest sister Darlee always made the mayonnaise for the salad. She would drop the oil in the egg mixture a few drops at the time. When the mayonnaise was about half done, she then begin a slow stream of oil to complete the mayonnaise. It would take 20 to 30 minutes to make. Today with a food processor it takes only 2 to 3 minutes, much easier and faster. The recipe makes 1½ cups mayonnaise.

6	eggs, in all	½	teaspoon white pepper
1	cup vegetable oil	5	cups water
2½	teaspoons salt, in all	3	pounds potatoes, peeled
1	tablespoon white vinegar		and diced

Place 2 eggs in food processor, processing until eggs begin to change to a light yellow color. Place oil in a measuring cup (to give control in adding oil to the feeding tube of the processor). Add in a slow stream for about 2 minutes. When mixture begins to thicken, add vinegar, ½ teaspoon salt and white pepper. Continue to process until mixture is to desired consistency. Place mixture into a medium bowl and set aside. In a 5-quart pot over high heat, place water and bring to a boil. Add remaining 2 teaspoons salt, potatoes and remaining 4 eggs. Cook 15 minutes or until potatoes are tender. Drain and add to bowl with mayonnaise. Peel eggs, chop and add to potato mixture, mixing well. "Good-good"

Chef Enola Prudhomme

Vegetable Medley

 *Makes 4 servings*

¼ cup butter or margarine	⅓ cup chopped fresh
½ cup broccoli flowerets	mushrooms
½ cup cauliflowerets	½ teaspoon vegetable
½ cup thinly sliced carrot	seasoning

In a medium skillet over high heat, melt butter. Combine broccoli, cauliflower, carrot, mushroom and seasoning. Cook and stir 3 minutes.

Chef Chris Oncale

Asparagus in Chablis

 Makes 4 servings

4 cups water	¼ teaspoon ground white pepper
1 pound fresh asparagus	
2 tablespoons butter or margarine	½ cup Chablis or other dry white wine
1 teaspoon salt	

In medium saucepan, bring 4 cups of water to a boil. Cut asparagus to 6-inch lengths from tip end and discard stems. Place asparagus in boiling water and blanch for 7 to 10 minutes. Remove asparagus from boiling water, set aside to cool and discard water. Melt butter or margarine in skillet over medium heat. Add asparagus, salt and white pepper. Cook about 1 minute. Add wine and cook 3 minutes. Serve hot.

Chef Donald Hebert

Black-eyed Peas

Makes 6 to 8 servings

 For a unique dish with the best flavor you have ever tasted, add the Country Fried Chicken recipe (found on page 122) to the black-eyed pea recipe and serve over rice. Also, if you don't have time to cook the dried beans, sauté the onion, bell pepper and 2 teaspoons of seasoning. Add 2 (16 ounce) cans of your favorite black-eyed peas and 1 cup of beef broth. Cook 10 minutes. Add the fried chicken; you'll love it!

9	cups water	½	cup finely chopped celery
1	pound dried black-eyed peas	1	cup finely chopped green bell pepper
2	bay leaves	1	cup finely chopped red bell pepper
2	tablespoons Enola's Special Seasoning	½	pound tasso, cut julienne
1	teaspoon salt	2	teaspoons minced garlic
1	cup finely chopped onion		

In a 5-quart pot over high heat, combine water, peas and bay leaves. Cook 1 hour. Add Enola's seasoning, salt, onion, celery, bell peppers, tasso and garlic. Cook 10 minutes, stirring occasionally. Reduce heat to medium, cover, and cook 30 minutes or until peas are tender, stirring occasionally. Remove bay leaves before serving.

Chef Enola Prudhomme

Fried Eggplant Rounds with Tasso Cream Sauce

Makes 4 servings

 This dish was a Gold Medal winner!

Eggplant:
¼	teaspoon salt	1	cup milk
¼	teaspoon ground red pepper	1	egg
¼	teaspoon ground black pepper	2	cups vegetable oil
1	large eggplant, peeled and cut in 1-inch slices	1	cup all-purpose flour
		1	cup dry bread crumbs

Cream Sauce:
1	tablespoon butter or margarine	¼	teaspoon ground white pepper
1	cup thinly sliced fresh mushrooms	¼	teaspoon ground red pepper
½	cup very finely chopped tasso	1	cup heavy whipping cream
¼	teaspoon salt	¼	cup finely chopped green onions

Eggplant:
In a small bowl, combine salt, red pepper and black pepper, mixing well. Sprinkle over both sides of eggplant slices. In a medium bowl, beat together milk and egg and set aside. In a large skillet over high heat, heat oil until very hot. Dredge each eggplant slice in flour, dip into milk and egg mixture, then dredge in bread crumbs. Carefully drop each eggplant slices in the hot oil and fry about 3 minutes or until golden brown. Remove from heat, place slices on paper towel to drain, set aside and keep warm.

Cream Sauce:
Melt butter or margarine in a heavy skillet over high heat. Add the mushrooms, tasso, salt, white pepper and red pepper. Cook and stir 5 minutes. Add the cream and cook and stir 5 minutes. Add the green onions and cook and stir an additional 2 minutes or until sauce thickens. To serve, place eggplant slices on a plate, and top with cream sauce. Serve hot.

Chef Enola Prudhomme

SAUCES & SPICES

Mushroom Sauce

 *Makes 6½ cups*

1 cup butter or margarine	1 cup (4 ounces) grated
3 cups finely chopped	Monterey Jack cheese
mushroom	1 cup (4 ounces) fresh grated
¼ cup chopped green onion	Parmesan cheese
½ cup all-purpose flour	1 teaspoon salt
1½ cups milk	2 teaspoons granulated garlic
1 (10½ ounce) can double rich	½ teaspoon ground white
beef broth	pepper
2 cups heavy whipping cream	1 tablespoon granulated onion
	½ cup white wine (optional)

In a heavy skillet oven high heat, melt butter. Add mushrooms and green onion. Cook and stir 5 minutes. Add the flour, 1 tablespoon at a time, stirring while adding the flour. Cook and stir 3 minutes. Add milk and broth. Cook and stir 5 minutes. Add the cream, both cheeses, salt, garlic, white pepper and granulated onion. Cook and stir an additional 5 minutes or until sauce thickens. Can be used with fish or chicken.

Chef Enola Prudhomme

Donald's Barbecue Sauce

Makes 3 cups

 Use this on chicken barbecued in the oven or over an outdoor pit.

½   cup butter or margarine
½   cup vegetable oil
4   cups finely chopped onion
½   cup finely chopped green
     bell pepper
1   lemon, quartered
1   (8 ounce) can tomato sauce

½   cup firmly packed light
     brown sugar
1   teaspoon salt
1   teaspoon garlic powder
1   teaspoon onion powder
¼   teaspoon ground red pepper
¼   teaspoon ground black
     pepper

In a 4-quart pot, combine all ingredients. Place over medium heat and cook 20 minutes, stirring occasionally. Remove lemon.

Chef Donald Hebert

Mom's Sweet Sauce

Makes 1 cup

 This sauce is great served over meat, poultry and also cake!

2	tablespoons freshly grated orange peel	¼	teaspoon ground allspice
½	cup orange juice	⅛	teaspoon salt
3	tablespoons red currant jelly	1	tablespoon cornstarch
½	cup raisins	½	cup water

In a medium saucepan over medium heat, combine orange peel, orange juice, jelly, raisins, allspice and salt. Cook and stir 15 minutes. Dissolve corn starch in water, add to saucepan and cook an additional 5 minutes.

Chef Enola Prudhomme

Lemon Butter Sauce

 Makes ½ cup

2	large lemons, (about ½ cup juice)
¼	cup butter or margarine
2	tablespoons vegetable oil
1	tablespoon Worcestershire sauce
½	teaspoon salt
2	teaspoons onion powder
2	teaspoons granulated garlic
2	teaspoons lemon zest

Squeeze lemon and set juice aside. In a small skillet over medium heat, melt butter. Add remaining ingredients and bring to boil. Serve over fish.

Chef Enola Prudhomme

Red Sauce for Meat or Seafood

 Makes 3 cups

3 tablespoons vegetable oil	½ teaspoon hot pepper sauce
1 cup finely chopped onion	1 teaspoon minced garlic
1 tablespoon plus 1 teaspoon paprika	1 teaspoon salt
3 tablespoons all-purpose flour	¼ teaspoon ground cumin
1 tablespoon plus 1 teaspoon chili powder	3 cups beef stock or broth

In a 5-quart pot over high heat, combine oil, onion and paprika. Cook and stir for 5 minutes. Add flour, 1 tablespoon at a time, stirring constantly. Reduce heat to medium. Add remaining ingredients. Cook, stirring occasionally, for 20 minutes. Can be cooked to reduce to 2 cups for a thicker richer sauce.

Chef Enola Prudhomme

Sonny's Barbecue Sauce

 *Makes 2½ cups*

1	cup butter or margarine	½	cup firmly packed brown sugar
2	cups coarsely chopped onion	1½	tablespoons mustard
½	cup coarsely chopped bell pepper	2	tablespoons Worcestershire sauce
¼	cup coarsely chopped celery	1	teaspoon salt
1	(8 ounce) can tomato sauce	½	teaspoon ground red pepper
½	cup ketchup	1	cup water
		½	teaspoon liquid hickory smoke

In a large pot over high heat, melt the butter. Add onion, bell pepper and celery. Cook until vegetables are transparent, about 10 minutes. Add remaining ingredients, stirring occasionally. Cook an additional 30 minutes or until sauce thickens.

Chef Sonny Aymond

Enola's Seasoning Recipe

 Makes 1 cup

4 tablespoons salt	3 tablespoons paprika
5 tablespoons plus 1 teaspoon granulated garlic	1 teaspoon ground white pepper
2 teaspoons ground black pepper	2 tablespoons dried oregano leaves
2 tablespoons granulated onion	2 tablespoons dried thyme leaves
2 teaspoons ground red pepper	

In a small bowl, combine all ingredients and mix well. Store in zip-lock bags or jars.

Chef Enola Prudhomme

Roux (In the Oven)

 Makes 5 cups

3 cups vegetable oil	¼ cup chopped celery
4½ cups all-purpose flour	1 teaspoon salt
1½ cups chopped onions	1 teaspoon ground red pepper
½ cup chopped green bell pepper	1 teaspoon garlic powder

Preheat oven to 350 degrees. Put oil in heavy oven-safe pot. Heat oil over high heat until oil smokes, about 10 minutes. Slowly add flour, stirring constantly. Cook 2 minutes, continuing to stir. Place pot in oven on center rack. Cook 25 minutes, stirring every 7 to 10 minutes. In a small bowl, mix onion, bell pepper, celery, salt, red pepper and garlic powder; add to roux and stir. Set aside to cool. For lighter roux, decrease cooking time; for darker roux increase cooking time. Unused roux can be stored in an air tight jar or container for several weeks.

Chef Donald Hebert

Pesto

Makes 4 servings

 This can be refrigerated for up to one week prior to using.

2 cups fresh basil leaves	1 cup freshly grated Parmesan cheese
½ cup roasted pecan pieces	
4 garlic cloves	2 teaspoons vegetable seasoning
1 cup olive oil	¼ cup warm water

In a food processor, combine basil leaves, pecans and garlic; process 30 seconds or until finely chopped. Continue to process and while machine is running, slowly add olive oil in a thin stream for 30 seconds. Stop processing and add cheese, seasoning and water. Press pulse button several times to combine. Serve over pasta.

Chef Enola Prudhomme

Homemade Curry Powder

 Makes ½ cup

4	teaspoons granulated garlic	1	teaspoon powdered ginger
4	teaspoons coriander seed	1	teaspoon fenugreek seed
3	teaspoons ground turmeric	1	teaspoon cardamon seed
1	teaspoon cumin seed	1	stick cinnamon
1	teaspoon white peppercorn	6	small dried chili peppers,
1	teaspoon mustard seed		with seeds

Place all ingredients in a blender container and process until all spices are evenly ground.

Chef Enola Prudhomme

DESSERTS
& BREADS

Coconut Cake

 Makes about 15 servings

Cake:
1	(15 ounce) pound cake mix	½	cup carbonated lemon-lime soda
3	eggs		
½	cup water		

Filling:
2	cups heavy whipping cream	2	tablespoons cornstarch
1	(15 ounce) can Coco Lopez	2½	cups shredded coconut

Frosting:
1	(8 ounce) package cream cheese, softened	1	(16 ounce) package powered sugar, sifted
½	cup butter or margarine, softened	1	teaspoon vanilla extract
		1½	cups flaked coconut

Cake:
Preheat oven to 350 degrees. In a medium bowl, combine the cake mix, eggs, water and soda, stirring well. Pour batter into 10-inch cake pan that have been greased and lined with wax paper. Bake 15 to 18 minutes or until cake tests done. Let cool on a wire rack, then cut cake in half horizontally to make 2 layers; and set aside.

Filling:
In a small sauce pan over medium heat, combine cream and coco lopez Bring to a boil, stirring constantly, being careful not to boil over. Reduce heat to simmer. Remove 1½ cups liquid. Dissolve cornstarch in liquid and set aside. Add 2 cups coconut to remaining liquid, cook and stir 3 minutes, remove from heat and set aside.

Frosting:
Combine cream cheese and butter or margarine, beating until smooth. Add powdered sugar and vanilla. Beat until light and fluffy.

Assemble:
Place half of the cake on a large cake board. Spoon half the reserved liquid over cake, then spoon half of coconut mixture over cake. Stack remaining half cake on top and repeat the process. Spread icing on all sides of cake. Sprinkle remaining coconut on top.

Chef Enola Prudhomme

Nutty Carrot Cake

 Makes 8 to 10 servings

Cake:

2	cups roasted pecans in all	2	cups sugar
4	eggs, beaten	1	teaspoon baking powder
¾	cup vegetable oil	1¾	teaspoons baking soda
2	teaspoons vanilla extract	3	cups grated carrots
½	teaspoon salt	2	cups all-purpose flour
½	teaspoon nutmeg	1	(6 ounce) can crushed
½	teaspoon ground cinnamon		pineapple in heavy syrup

Syrup:

1	cup milk	1	teaspoon vanilla extract
½	cup sugar		

Frosting:

1	(8 ounce) package cream cheese, softened	1	(16 ounce) package powdered sugar
½	cup butter or margarine, softened	1	teaspoon vanilla extract
		1	cup very finely chopped pecans

Chantilly Cream:

4	cups heavy whipping cream	2	teaspoons vanilla extract, rum or brandy
2	cups sugar		

Cake:
Preheat oven to 350 degrees. Place pecans in food processor and process until finely chopped. Set aside. In a medium bowl, combine eggs, oil, vanilla, salt, nutmeg and cinnamon. Beat with a hand mixer at medium speed 3 minutes. Add sugar, baking powder, baking soda and carrots. Beat at high speed 2 minutes. Add flour, pineapple with juice and 1 cup pecans. Beat an additional 2 minutes or until batter is nice and fluffy. Spoon batter into three 9-inch oiled and floured round cake pans. Bake 30 minutes or until cake is done; test by inserting a wooden toothpick in the center and if it comes out clean, the cake should be fully baked. Cool 10 minutes, then place on wire rack, cool 10 minutes longer, and then transfer to a cake board.

(Nutty Carrot Cake continued on next page)

(Nutty Carrot Cake continued)

Syrup:
In a sauce pan, combine milk, sugar and vanilla. Place over high heat, bring to a boil and cook, stirring constantly, 5 minutes. Remove from heat and set aside. Spoon over cake layers before using frosting.

Frosting:
Combine cream cheese and butter or margarine, beating until smooth. Add powdered sugar, extract and pecans. Beat at medium speed until mixture is light and fluffy. Spread icing evenly over the entire cake.

Chantilly Cream:
In a medium bowl, combine cream, sugar and vanilla, rum or brandy. With a hand mixer on high speed, mix until nice and fluffy or until cream comes to a peak. Cut cake and place a slice on a plate. Spoon chantilly over cake and serve with milk or coffee. M-m-m-good!

Chef Enola Prudhomme

Carrot Cake

 Makes 12 to 14 servings

Cake:

4	eggs
2	cups sugar
1	cup vegetable oil
2¼	cups all-purpose flour
2	teaspoons baking soda
1	teaspoon baking powder
1	teaspoon salt

1 (8 ounce) package cream cheese, softened
½ cup butter or margarine, melted
1 (16 ounce) package

2½ teaspoons ground cinnamon
2 cups chopped pecans, in all
2 cups grated carrots
1 (8 ounce) can crushed pineapple in heavy syrup

Frosting:

powdered sugar, sifted
1 teaspoon vanilla extract

Cake:

Preheat oven to 375 degrees. Beat eggs and add sugar. Gradually stir in oil. Mix with dry ingredients. Add 1 cup chopped pecans. Fold in carrots and pineapple. Pour batter into two 9-inch round cake pans that have been greased with oil and floured. Bake 35 minutes or until top of cake springs back when touched. Place remaining 1 cup pecans in a food processor and press pulse button 4 to 5 time to chop. Pecans should be the size of raw rice.

Frosting:
Combine cream cheese and butter or margarine, beating until smooth. Add powdered sugar and vanilla. Beat until light and fluffy. Add chopped pecans and stir well to mix. Spread mixture over 1 layer of cake, top with second layer and then spread frosting over the entire cake.

Chef Enola Prudhomme

Pound Cake

 *Makes 10 servings*

1 cup butter or margarine, softened	5 eggs
	1½ teaspoons lemon extract
2 cups sugar	1½ teaspoons almond extract
2 cups all-purpose flour	

Preheat oven to 350 degrees. In a medium bowl, cream butter or margarine and sugar with a hand mixer on medium speed for 5 minutes. Add flour, eggs, lemon and almond extract, mixing thoroughly. Pour mixture into a greased and floured fluted tube pan. Bake 45 minutes to 1 hour, checking with toothpick by sticking in center; when toothpick comes out clean cake is done. Let cool 10 to 15 minutes.

Chef Sonny Aymond

Punch Bowl Cake

Makes 8 servings

 I could not find fresh strawberries so I used frozen strawberries for this recipe. Of course, fresh is always better and if they are available in your area, by all means use them. Simply slice the fresh strawberries and add the sugar. This is a delicious dish you will want to make often.

1	pound fresh or frozen strawberries, thawed	2	bananas, peeled and thinly sliced
½	cup sugar	1	pound cake, cut into bite-size pieces
1	(3.4 ounce) package instant pistachio pudding mix	1	(12 ounce) container frozen whipped topping, thawed
2	cups evaporated milk		

If you use frozen berries: In a small saucepan over medium heat, combine the strawberries and sugar. Cook and stir 5 minutes and set aside. In a medium bowl, combine the pudding mix and milk. Beat 5 minutes or until pudding starts to thicken, and set aside. In a glass bowl, layer half of the pound cake, half of pudding, 1 banana, half of whipped topping and most of strawberries; repeat the process with the remaining ingredients, ending with the whipped topping. Garnish with remaining strawberries. If strawberries are not available, use cherries with mint leaves.

Chef Enola Prudhomme

Four Day Coconut Cake

Makes 8 servings

 This cake is exceptionally moist because it absorbs the sour cream filling over a four-day period of time.

1	(18½ ounce) package yellow cake mix	1	cup sugar
2	cups sour cream	1	(24 ounce) package flaked coconut

Prepare cake according to package directions, making two layers. Split each layer to make four layers. In a medium bowl, combine sour cream, sugar and coconut, mixing well. Spread between cake layers and on top but not on sides. Seal in covered cake container and refrigerate for 4 days.

Chef Donald Hebert

Carrot Pineapple Cupcakes

 *Makes 12*

1 cup all-purpose flour	⅛ teaspoon salt
⅓ cup sugar	1 egg, beaten
1 teaspoon baking powder	¼ cup vegetable oil
½ teaspoon soda	1 cup shredded carrots
1 teaspoon ground cinnamon	½ cup crushed pineapple,
¼ teaspoon ground nutmeg	drained
	1 teaspoon vanilla extract

Preheat oven to 350 degrees. Place paper baking cups in muffin tins. In a large mixing bowl, mix flour, sugar, baking powder, baking soda, cinnamon, nutmeg and salt. Stir in egg, oil, carrots, pineapple and vanilla. Spoon batter into paper-lined muffin tins. Bake 20 minutes or until tops of cup cakes spring back when touched lightly. Cool on a wire rack before serving.

Chef Donald Hebert

Cheesecake

 *Makes 8 servings*

Crust:

1¼ cups graham cracker crumbs

2 tablespoons butter or margarine, melted

2 tablespoons sugar

Filling:

3 (8 ounce) packages cream cheese, softened

4 eggs, at room temperature

1 cup sugar

¼ cup processed cheese spread

Topping:

2 cups sour cream

1½ teaspoons vanilla extract

2 tablespoons sugar

Crust:
In a medium bowl, combine crumbs, butter or margarine and sugar, mixing well. Place in a 9-inch pie plate. With a fork, press mixture evenly around plate.

Filling:
Combine cream cheese and eggs, mixing well. Add sugar and cheese spread. Beat at low speed for 15 minutes. Pour filling into prepared crust. Bake at 350 degrees for 20 minutes.

Topping:
In a medium bowl, mix sour cream, vanilla and sugar. Beat 1 minute with a hand mixer. Spread topping evenly over cake and bake an additional 8 minutes. Remove from oven and refrigerate to chill.

Chef Donald Hebert

Pastry from Double Crust Pie

 Makes 1 crust

2	cups all-purpose flour	7	tablespoons ice cold water
1	tablespoon salt	2	tablespoons milk
⅔	cup vegetable shortening		

Preheat oven to 350 degrees. In a medium mixing bowl, combine flour and salt. With a pastry cutter, cut in shortening until mixture resembles rice. Add water and mix with hands until dough holds together and can be rolled easily; be careful not to overwork the dough. Separate dough into two equal portions. Roll out half the dough on a floured surface; repeat for the second crust and set aside. Place circle of dough in a 9-inch pie pan, overlapping approximately 1-inch around rim. Trim excess dough from edges. Prick the bottom of the pie crust with the tines of a fork to allow the moisture to escape. Fill pie shell with your favorite filling until ¾ full. Place second dough circle over filling. Press edges of dough together with your finger tips to seal the pie. Cut 2 to 3-inch slits on the top of the pie to allow moisture to escape. This will make a nice crispy crust. Bake 15 to 20 minutes or until golden brown.

Chef Donald Hebert

Chocolate Praline Pie

 Makes 8 servings

3	eggs, beaten	1	cup pecan halves
1	cup light corn syrup	¾	cup semi-sweet chocolate
½	cup sugar		chips, in all
⅓	cup butter or margarine	1	unbaked 9-inch pie shell
2	tablespoons praline liqueur or Amaretto		

Preheat oven to 350 degrees. In a medium mixing bowl, slightly beat eggs with a hand mixer. Add corn syrup, sugar, butter or margarine and liqueur. Stir constantly until sugar is dissolved. Add pecan halves and ½ cup chocolate chips. Spoon into pie shell. Cover edges with aluminum foil to prevent burning. Bake 25 minutes. Remove foil, sprinkle remaining chocolate chips on top of pie and bake an additional 20 to 25 minutes or until knife tip inserted near center comes out clean. Do not overbake. Cool thoroughly before serving.

Chef Donald Hebert

Deep Dish Apple Pie

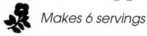 *Makes 6 servings*

2	medium-sized red apples	½	cup apple juice
2	tablespoons lemon juice	1¼	cups sugar
2	eggs	1½	cups all-purpose flour
¼	teaspoon vanilla extract	½	cup heavy whipping cream
¼	teaspoon ground nutmeg	2	(9-inch) unbaked pie crusts
¼	teaspoon ground cinnamon		

Preheat oven to 375 degrees. Peel apples and slice thinly. Add lemon juice, toss and set aside. Beat the eggs until frothy. Add vanilla, nutmeg and cinnamon. Whip until mixed. Add apple juice and sugar. Blend in flour and whipping cream. In a deep dish pie pan, roll dough to fit bottom and side. Add the apple slices and egg mixture. Cut the remaining pie dough in strips and crisscross over filling to make the top crust. Press around edges. Bake 30 minutes, increase oven temperature to 400 degrees and bake 30 minutes or until nice and browned.

Chef Enola Prudhomme

Peach Cobbler

 *Makes 8 servings*

Batter:

1	(29 ounce) can sliced peaches in heavy syrup	½	cup heavy cream
2	cups biscuit mix	⅓	cup peach juice
½	cup sugar	½	cup butter milk

Filling:

1	cup buttermilk	1	cup sugar
1	cup heavy whipping cream	2	cups chopped peaches
2	tablespoons butter or margarine	4	tablespoons cornstarch
1	cup peach juice	¼	cup water

Batter:
Drain peaches, reserving liquid, and set peaches aside for filling. In a medium bowl, combine biscuit mix, sugar, cream, peach juice, and buttermilk. Mix for 1 minute and set aside.

Filling:
Preheat oven to 425 degrees. In a 4-quart saucepan over high heat, combine buttermilk, cream, butter or margarine, peach juice and sugar. Bring to a boil and add peaches. In a small cup, combine cornstarch and water, mixing well. Add to boiling mixture. Cook for 1 minute, then remove from heat and set aside. Spray a 13x9x2-inch baking pan with nonstick spray. Pour ⅔ of the batter into pan, spread ⅔ of the filling over batter and layer remaining batter over filling. Bake 25 minutes. Pour the remaining filling over cobbler for extra flavor.

Chef Chris Oncale

Beau's Easy Bread Pudding

 Makes 10 servings

5 eggs	2½ cups milk
1½ cups sugar	½ cup margarine, melted and
1 teaspoon vanilla extract	cooled
½ teaspoon ground nutmeg	6 cups day-old toast or bread
½ teaspoon ground cinnamon	½ cup chopped pecans

Preheat oven to 375 degrees. In a medium bowl, beat together eggs, sugar, vanilla, nutmeg, cinnamon, milk and margarine with a wire whisk. Tear bread into bite-sized pieces and add to milk mixture along with pecans. Let soak for 20 minutes. Spray a 12x9x2-inch baking dish with nonstick cooking spray. Spoon in bread mixture. Bake for 35 minutes or until top is golden brown.

Chef Sonny Aymond

Drunken Banana Pudding

 Makes 10 (½ cup) servings

2 (3.4 ounce) packages instant banana cream pudding mix	1 (20 ounce) package vanilla wafers
3½ cups milk	5 bananas, peeled and thinly sliced
½ cup light rum, optional	
1 teaspoon vanilla extract	

In a large bowl, combine pudding mix, milk, rum and vanilla. Beat until smooth. Line the bottom of a 12x9x2-inch baking dish with a layer of vanilla wafers. Top with a layer of bananas and half of the pudding, spreading evenly. Line sides of dish with vanilla wafers. Arrange another layer of vanilla wafers on pudding and top with layer of bananas and the remaining pudding, spreading evenly. Chill for one hour.

Chef Donald Hebert

Prudhomme's Bread Pudding

Makes 6 to 8 servings

12 cups day-old white bread or French bread	1 teaspoon ground cinnamon
3 eggs	1 teaspoon ground nutmeg
2 cups sugar	2 teaspoons vanilla extract
2 cups canned evaporated milk	½ cup raisins
1 cup water	½ cup pecan pieces
	2 tablespoons butter or margarine

Preheat oven to 350 degrees. Cut or tear bread into cubes and set aside. In a medium bowl, beat the eggs. Combine sugar, milk, water, cinnamon, nutmeg, vanilla, raisins and pecans. Stir until smooth. Add milk mixture to cubed bread and mix well. Let stand at least 1 hour or until bread soaks up liquid. Pour mixture into oiled 13x9x2-inch baking pan. Cut butter or margarine into small cubes and dot over bread mixture. Bake 30 minutes or until bread pudding is firm.

Chef Enola Prudhomme

Chantilly Cream

 Makes 1½ quarts

4   cups heavy whipping cream, very cold
¼   cup sugar

2   teaspoons vanilla extract or 1 tablespoon Irish cream liqueur

Place plastic portion of food processor in freezer for about ½ hour or until cold. Remove from freezer, then place on processor motor. Combine cream, sugar and extract or liqueur in food processor. Beat until cream forms a peak. Serve over hot bread budding or any flavored cake. Also tastes good in hot coffee or chocolate.

Chef Enola Prudhomme

No-Bake Candy Fruit Cake

 Makes 4 to 6 servings

1	(13 ounce) can condensed milk	1	cup chopped pecans
2	cups graham crackers	1	cup candied fruits

In a medium bowl, combine all ingredients, mixing well. Shape mixture into a roll about the size of a 50-cent piece and 12-inches long. Wrap in clear plastic wrap and chill 1 hour. Slice and serve.

Chef Donald Hebert

Gingerbread Cookies

 *Makes 24*

½ cup butter or margarine, softened	1½ cups sugar
1 cup dark molasses	2¼ teaspoons baking soda
2 eggs	1 teaspoon salt
⅓ cup water	4 teaspoons ground cinnamon
5 cups all-purpose flour	2 teaspoons ground ginger
	1 teaspoon ground cloves

Preheat oven to 350 degrees. In a medium bowl, cream butter or margarine and sugar. Add molasses and eggs. Stir in the water. Mix flour, sugar, baking soda, salt, cinnamon, ginger and cloves together, then add to the egg mixture, stirring well. Chill dough at least 1 hour. Roll the dough on a floured surface to ¼-inch thickness. Cut into desired shapes and place on baking sheets. Bake 7 to 10 minutes.

Chef Donald Hebert

Fig Cookies

 *Makes 40*

1	cup sugar	2½	cups all-purpose flour
1	cup firmly packed brown sugar	1	teaspoon baking powder
1	cup butter or margarine, softened	1	teaspoon baking soda
2	eggs, beaten	1	teaspoon vanilla extract
		3	cups chopped figs

Preheat oven to 350 degrees. In a medium bowl, combine sugar, brown sugar, butter or margarine, eggs, flour, baking powder, baking soda and vanilla, mixing well. Stir in the figs. Drop dough by tablespoonfuls on greased baking sheet, spacing 1-inch apart. Bake 13 to 15 minutes or until cookies are golden brown.

Chef Chris Oncale

Chris's Gold Medal Winner Cajun Crunch

 Makes 8 to 10 servings

2 dozen day-old muffins	2 cups chopped pecans
2 cups sugar	2 cups milk
1⅓ cups chocolate chips	2 cups heavy whipping cream
2 (3.4 ounce) packages instant chocolate pudding mix	1 teaspoon butter-flavor extract
1 (21.4 ounce) package cheese cake mix	½ cup water
	2 cups chocolate syrup

Preheat oven to 350 degrees. In a large bowl, crumble muffins. Add sugar, chocolate chips, pudding mix, cheesecake mix and pecans, blending. Add milk, cream, extract and water, mixing well. Spoon mixture into a 9x9x2-inch baking dish. Bake 40 minutes or until firm. Top with chocolate syrup and cut into equal squares.

Chef Chris Oncale

Cloud for Cajun Crunch

 Makes 8 to 10 servings

4	cups heavy whipping cream	2	teaspoons vanilla extract
2	cups sugar		

In a blender, combine cream, sugar and vanilla. Blend until thick. Keep chilled. Serve as cloud over Cajun Crunch or other favorite dessert.

Chef Chris Oncale

Peanut Butter Chocolate Kisses

Makes 36

 Nicole Bernard, a co-worker of my wife, baked these cookies and brought them to our home as a "get well" gift. This recipe was handed down by her mother. Peanut butter cookies are a family favorite at our home, especially when sealed with a kiss! That's what friends are for. Thanks Nicole!

1½ **cups sugar, in all**	¼ **cup vegetable shortening**
½ **cup firmly packed brown**	1 **egg, beaten**
sugar	1½ **cups all-purpose flour**
½ **cup peanut butter**	¾ **teaspoon baking soda**
¼ **cup butter or margarine,**	½ **teaspoon baking powder**
softened	36 **chocolate kisses**

Preheat oven to 375 degrees. In a large bowl, combine 1 cup sugar, brown sugar, peanut butter, butter or margarine, shortening and egg. Stir in flour, soda and baking powder. Shape into 1-inch balls. Roll in remaining ½ cup sugar. Place about 2-inches apart on ungreased baking sheet. Bake 8 to 12 minutes or until edges are golden brown. Remove from oven and press chocolate kiss firmly in center of each cookie. Let cool and enjoy!

Chef Sonny Aymond

Sweet and Simple Snack

Makes 24

 This recipe is a great for breakfast or after school snack!

1	cup sugar	2	cups pancake mix
1	teaspoon cinnamon	1½	cup milk
1	teaspoon nutmeg	1	cup vegetable oil
8	slices toast		

In a small bowl, mix sugar, cinnamon and nutmeg; set aside. Cut bread lengthwise into 1½-inch pieces and set aside. In a medium bowl, combine pancake mix, milk and half of the sugar mixture. Stir mixture until smooth. Dip each piece of bread into the batter; let excess batter drain off. In a medium skillet over high heat, add a few pieces of bread at a time and fry in oil 2 to 3 minutes or until golden brown on both sides. Remove from the skillet and place on a paper towel to drain. Sprinkle the remaining sugar mixture over the bread. Serve with cold milk or a cup of your favorite coffee.

Chef Enola Prudhomme

Ike's Sweet Potato Muffins

 Makes about 16

2 cups all-purpose flour	½ cup chopped raisins
1¼ cups grated, peeled sweet potato	¼ cup chopped walnuts or pecans
1 cup sugar	2 large eggs
2 teaspoons baking powder	1 cup milk
1 teaspoon ground cinnamon	½ cup unsalted butter or margarine, melted and
¼ teaspoon salt	cooled
¼ teaspoon freshly grated nutmeg	

Preheat oven to 350 degrees. In a large bowl, whisk together the flour, sweet potatoes, sugar, baking powder, cinnamon, salt, nutmeg, raisins and walnuts. In another bowl, whisk together the eggs, milk and butter or margarine. Stir the egg mixture into the flour mixture, mixing just until dry ingredients are moistened. Spoon batter into greased muffin tins. Bake 30 minutes or until golden brown.

Chef Ike Broussard

Banana Nut Bread

Makes one loaf

 This bread is great served warm or cold.

½	cup butter or margarine, softened	2	tablespoons boiling water
1	cup sugar	2	eggs, beaten
2	large ripe bananas, peeled and mashed	1	teaspoon lemon juice
1	tablespoon baking powder	½	cup chopped pecans or walnuts
		2	cups all-purpose flour
		¼	teaspoon ground nutmeg

Preheat oven to 350 degrees. In a medium bowl, combine butter or margarine and sugar. Cream with mixer on high speed. Stir in bananas and set aside. Place baking soda in boiling water and stir until dissolved. Add soda liquid to margarine mixture along with eggs, lemon juice, nuts, flour and nutmeg, stirring well. Pour the batter into a 8x4x2-inch loaf pan that has been sprayed with vegetable cooking spray. Bake 1 hour.

Chef Donald Hebert

Quick Buttermilk Biscuits

Makes 4 to 6 servings

 Coming from a large family, my mom sometimes did not have time to roll out the biscuits. So she would just spoon the dough into a baking dish, bake and cut each of us a square out of the dish. She called this a biscuit tout de suite or "quick quick".

2½ cups all-purpose flour	¼ cup chilled vegetable
1 tablespoon baking powder	shortening
½ teaspoon baking soda	1½ cups buttermilk
1 teaspoon salt	

Preheat oven to 375 degrees. In a large bowl, combine flour, baking powder, baking soda and salt, mixing well. Using a pastry blender, cut in shortening until coarse crumbs form. Add buttermilk. Dough will be thin. Spoon into greased 8x8x2-inch baking pan. Bake for 20 minutes or until golden brown. Cut into squares.

Chef Enola Prudhomme

Jalapeño and Cheese Muffins

Makes 16

½ cup fresh jalapeño peppers	2 cups milk
2 cups yellow corn meal	2 eggs, beaten
¼ cup plus 2 teaspoons sugar	½ cup liquid shortening
2 cups all-purpose flour	1½ cups (6 ounces) shredded
½ teaspoons salt	cheddar cheese

Preheat oven to 375 degrees. Using rubber gloves, wash and pat dry the jalapeños. Remove the seeds, mince and set aside. In a medium bowl, combine corn meal, sugar, flour and salt, mixing well. In a small bowl and using a wire whisk, combine eggs and milk, beating well. Slowly add to the dry ingredients, stirring well. Add oil, cheese and peppers, stirring well. Spread a few drops of oil in each muffin tin with finger tips. With a spoon or a medium ice cream scoop, fill each muffin cup ¾ full. Bake 20 minutes or until golden brown.

Chef Enola Prudhomme

Fresh Blueberry Jam

Makes 5 (½ pint) jars

 Tip: Don't use over ripe fruit or pectin will have to be added!

3   pounds blueberries, crushed   **½   teaspoon lemon juice**
4½ cups sugar

In an 8-quart sauce pan, combine berries, sugar and lemon juice. Bring to a boil and cook, at 220 degrees, about 15 minutes, stirring constantly. In a 5-quart pot, bring water to boil. Place jars and lids in boiling water to sterilize, then carefully remove from pot. Add jam to hot jars, leaving a ¼-inch space for expansion. Place hot lids and rings onto jars and screw tightly. Place filled jars back in boiling water for 5 minutes to process. Remove jars and let cool. Enjoy!

Chef Chris Oncale

Strawberry Fig Preserves

 Makes 5 (½ pint) jars

3 cups fresh figs	2 ½ cups sugar
2 (3 ounce) packages strawberry gelatin	Water

Mix figs, gelatin and sugar in large saucepan. Bring to a boil and cook for about 20 minutes, stirring occasionally. In a 5-quart pot over high heat, bring water to boil. Place jars and lids in boiling water to sterilize. Remove from pot. Add preserves to hot jar, leaving ¼-inch space for expansion. Place hot lids and rings on jars and screw tightly. Place filled jars back in boiling water for 5 minutes to process.

Chef Donald Hebert

INDEX

R

S

 **Notes**

Enola Prudhomme

4676 NE Evangeline Thruway
Carencro, LA 70520

Please send _____ copies   @ $17.95 each _____

Louisiana residents add sales tax   @ $ 1.26 each _____

Postage and handling   @ $ 3.00 each _____

                                                              Total _____

Name _____

Address _____

City _____ State _____ Zip _____

Make checks payable to Enola Prudhomme

Enola Prudhomme

4676 NE Evangeline Thruway
Carencro, LA 70520

Please send _____ copies   @ $17.95 each _____

Louisiana residents add sales tax   @ $ 1.26 each _____

Postage and handling   @ $ 3.00 each _____

                                                              Total _____

Name _____

Address _____

City _____ State _____ Zip _____

Make checks payable to Enola Prudhomme